JESUS GOD and MAN

JESUS GOD AND MAN is one of the volumes in the series, IMPACT BOOKS, designed to bring the modern reader the significant achievements of scholars, both Catholic and non-Catholic, in the fields of Scripture, Theology, Philosophy, Mathematics, History, and the Physical and Social Sciences. Among the titles in the series are:

JESUS
GOD and MAN

Modern Biblical Reflections

by RAYMOND E. BROWN, S.S.

MACMILLAN PUBLISHING CO., INC.

NEW YORK

COLLIER MACMILLAN PUBLISHERS

LONDON

NIHIL OBSTAT:

John A. Schulien, S.T.D.
Censor librorum

IMPRIMATUR:

✠ William E. Cousins
Archbishop of Milwaukee
July 24, 1967

The Nihil obstat and Imprimatur are a declaration that a book or pamphlet is considered to be free from doctrinal or moral error. It is not implied that those who have granted the Nihil obstat and Imprimatur agree with the contents, opinions, or statements expressed.

MACMILLAN PUBLISHING CO., INC.
866 THIRD AVENUE, NEW YORK, N.Y. 10022
COLLIER MACMILLAN CANADA, INC.

Library of Congress Catalog Card Number: 67–29587

17   16   15   14   13   12   11

PRINTED IN THE UNITED STATES OF AMERICA

To
FATHER JAMES A. LAUBACHER, S.S.
Rector of St. Patrick's Seminary, California

With gratitude, shared by so many, for his thirty years of
devoted service to St. Mary's Seminary, Baltimore
and with personal gratitude for all that I have received
from him as teacher, rector, counselor and friend.

Abbreviations

OLD TESTAMENT

Gn	Genesis	Lam	Lamentations
Ex	Exodus	Ez	Ezekiel
Lv	Leviticus	Dn	Daniel
Nm	Numbers	Hos	Hosea
Dt	Deuteronomy	Jl	Joel
Jos	Joshua	Amos	Amos
Jg	Judges	Ob	Obadiah
Ru	Ruth	Jon	Jonah
1, 2 Sm	1, 2 Samuel	Mi	Micah
1, 2 Kg	1, 2 Kings	Na	Nahum
1, 2 Chr	1, 2 Chronicles	Hb	Habakkuk
Ezr	Ezra	Zeph	Zephaniah
Neh	Nehemiah	Hg	Haggai
Est	Esther	Ze	Zechariah
Jb	Job	Mal	Malachi
Ps	Psalms	Bar	Baruch
Prv	Proverbs	Tob	Tobit
Qoh	Qoheleth	Jud	Judith
	(Ecclesiastes)	Wis	Wisdom of Solomon
Ct	Song of Songs	Sir	Ben Sira
Is	Isaiah		(Ecclesiasticus)
Jer	Jeremiah	1, 2 Mac	1, 2 Maccabees

NEW TESTAMENT

Mt	Matthew	Col	Colossians
Mk	Mark	1, 2 Th	1, 2 Thessalonians
Lk	Luke	1, 2 Tim	1, 2 Timothy
Jn	John	Tit	Titus
Acts	Acts	Phm	Philemon
Rom	Romans	Heb	Hebrews
1, 2 Cor	1, 2 Corinthians	Jas	James
Gal	Galatians	1, 2 Pt	1, 2 Peter
Eph	Ephesians	1, 2, 3 Jn	1, 2, 3 John
Phil	Philippians	Jude	Jude
		Ap	Apocalypse

Other Abbreviations

BASOR = *Bulletin of the American Schools of Oriental Research*

DBS = *Enchiridion Symbolorum*, 32nd edition, revised Denzinger's by A. Schönmetzer (Freiburg: Herder, 1963).

VDBS = *Supplément au Dictionnaire de la Bible* (Vigouroux)

PL = Migne's *Patrologia Latina*

PG = Migne's *Patrologia Graeca*

Preface

In A.D. 325 the Council of Nicaea solemnly defined the divinity of Jesus; in 451 the Council of Chalcedon solemnly defined his full humanity (in everything except sin). Since that time the Church has stubbornly reaffirmed against all opponents her faith that Jesus is true God and true man. There has been much opposition to each of these truths, opposition that has arisen respectively in different ways. Opposition to the belief that Jesus is true God has been more articulate in scholarly circles: philosophers, scientists, historians of religion, and biblical critics have at one time or another rejected the divinity of Jesus as impossible or as popular legend. For that reason, in her public statements about the incarnation the Church has had to be insistent on the divinity of Jesus — a necessary situation that has had the unfortunate side effect of creating the impression that divinity is the only important issue. Yet there is also widespread opposition to the humanity of Jesus, an opposition that is often neglected because it is unconscious or not formally articulated. Many Christian believers do not sufficiently appreciate the humanity of Jesus. They transfer the picture of the glorified Jesus back into his public ministry, imagining him to have walked through Galilee with an aura and a halo about him. They cannot imagine him as being like other men; and they are embarrassed by the Gospel vignettes of Jesus as sometimes tired and dirty, annoyed and tempted, indistinguishable in a crowd, treated as a fanatic and a rabble-rouser. How pervasive is this attitude toward the humanity of Jesus becomes evident in the vociferous opposition to any new translation of the Gospels that strips away the hallowed jargon of "Bible English" and has Jesus speak in an everyday manner.

In our own generation the unending struggle to preserve the twofold truth about Christ is inevitably affected by the Church's acceptance of modern biblical criticism, an acceptance that in Roman Catholic circles has taken place in the past twenty years and whose impact will be felt keenly in the years to come. Perhaps in this day of exaggerated advertising it would be wise to caution from the first that I do not mean that biblical criticism will or can cause the Church to reject what was proclaimed at Nicaea or at Chalcedon. But this criticism can make us better understand the implications of those proclamations and what they did and did not settle. Too often in Catholic theological circles biblical criticism is treated as if it were frosting on the cake — it looks nice and lends a scientific flavor, but it does not affect fundamentals. But we cannot compartmentalize our knowledge and our faith into hermetically sealed units. The belief that Jesus is God and man involves a whole complex of understanding, a complex in which the biblical evidence has a very important formative role.

The first chapter in this book is concerned with an aspect of the contribution that the biblical evidence makes toward our understanding of Jesus' divinity. Commenting in general here, we note that this contribution is in terms of historical consciousness, which is a distinctive mark of all modern critical study. By historical consciousness we mean the awareness that there is a constant interplay between human knowledge and the times and conditions in which that knowledge is gained. In ages past some scholars already gave evidence of historical consciousness; but in the last two centuries, more than at any other time, we have become acutely aware that our knowledge is not eternal. What we know is phrased in the terms and concepts of a particular time and in light of a particular problematic. Therefore, to understand what was being affirmed at any past era it is not enough simply to recite the formulas of that era; one must know what those formulas meant to the men who uttered them, realizing that the same formula uttered at different times may have different meanings. To judge how much truth those formulas contain one must take into account the limited perspective of the men who formulated them (as well as our own limited perspective in investigating the problem). Opposed to this approach is a type of fundamentalism that sees human formulations of truth as independent of space and time. In the particular area of the Christian religion this fundamentalism becomes an acute problem when it is maintained against the background of the axiom that divine public revelation came to a close with the death of the last apostle (an axiom which, it may be said in passing, is frequently misinterpreted). To the fundamentalist, this means that all the Christian dogmas from the divinity of Christ to the Assumption of Mary were known in apostolic times, and thus the development of doctrine consists merely in drawing forth from the deposit of faith (conceived of in the manner of a bank deposit) the already formulated answers to problems that should never have arisen. For the historically conscious scholar, however, the problems that arose are precisely what brought really new insights and caused the Church to formulate her thought in a way not hitherto done. It is quite true, of course, that a new formulation need not reflect the grasp of an entirely new truth; often a new formulation is an almost instinctive reaction in order to defend a truth that was previously accepted in a general and undifferentiated way but is now imperiled. Nevertheless, a new formulation means at least a new precision that was not there before; and to that extent one's thought is different from, even if in continuity with, the thought of the past.

In the case of the divinity of Jesus, an era of fundamentalist apologetics that was not historically conscious simply read both the formulation and the problematic of Nicaea back into the New Testament period (despite the explicit admission of Athanasius, the greatest of the Nicene Fathers, that in its formulation Nicaea was going beyond anything said explicitly in the New Testament). Because Nicaea called Jesus God, some apologists assumed that the disciples must have called Jesus God even during his ministry! The impact of biblical criticism on this point is already apparent in the April 21, 1964 Instruction of the Pontifical Biblical Commission, which implies that it was only after the resurrection that the disciples perceived Jesus' divinity.[1] But even this recognition does not do full justice to the problem of development. In what sense did they recognize his divinity? In 2 Cor 5:19 Paul says that "God was in Christ reconciling the world to Himself"; this is scarcely the same as saying that Christ was God. Our first chapter raises the question: "Does the New Testament call Jesus God?" and seeks to trace a development in the formulation of this question in the New Testament. Hopefully it makes clear how the problematic of the New Testament differed from that of Nicaea.

The second chapter is concerned with an aspect of the contribution that the biblical evidence makes toward our

---

[1] *Catholic Biblical Quarterly* 26 (1964) 307: "After Jesus had risen from the dead and when his divinity was clearly perceived . . . "

understanding of Jesus' humanity. Nowhere does the problem about the reality and fullness of Jesus' humanity appear more clearly than in the question of how much knowledge Jesus possessed. For hundreds of years theologians, thoroughly convinced of the truth of Chalcedon, have nevertheless insisted that Jesus was not human to the extent of ignorance. They have based their conclusions on a priori reasoning from the fact of the hypostatic union, emphasizing that a *divine* person possessed the human nature. The biblical evidence was interpreted in the light of these conclusions and made to fit them (a feat that was not too difficult before the advent of modern criticism). Recently, the thesis of the omniscience of Jesus (absolute, or just in religious matters) has been challenged by other theologians, but also on the basis of a priori reasoning. Even though these theologians were more aware of the biblical evidence than their predecessors, their main arguments have still been drawn from the effects of the hypostatic union. Without attempting to solve this problem — which goes far beyond the field of Scripture — I have gathered the biblical evidence and discussed it in terms of modern critical exegesis, so that all may see the a posteriori situation. Hopefully, this biblical evidence will not only serve as the raw material from which to formulate a solution but will also color and shape the solution. If it does that, it will cease to be the frosting on the cake.

These two chapters were the product of a christological study that I did in the summer of 1965, prompted by experiences in teaching the biblical background of a course on the Trinity while the professor of that course was at the Vatican Council. Because of various circumstances the two chapters were published separately a year and a half

apart and then only partially.[2] I am grateful to The Bruce
Publishing Company for bringing them back together
again in full so that they may be of greater service for those
who wish to study the question of Jesus God and man.
They treat only facets of the problem; but if they are
understood, the method of treating other facets should be
much clearer.

[2] The first was published in *Theological Studies* 26 (1965) 545–573;
the second in part in *Catholic Biblical Quarterly* 29 (1967) 315–345.
The publishers are grateful to these periodicals for the permission to
reprint.

Contents

JESUS GOD and MAN

CHAPTER ONE

Does The New Testament
Call Jesus God?

This chapter has a very limited goal; perhaps we can best make this clear by stating what the chapter does *not* intend to discuss. First, this chapter will not raise the question of whether Jesus was God. This question was settled for the Church at Nicaea, where it was clearly confessed that the Son was God and not a creature; he was "true God of true God." The recognition that such a belief is still the hallmark of the true Christian is found in the Amsterdam Confession of the World Council of Churches, which stated that the World Council is composed of "Churches which acknowledge Jesus Christ as God and Savior." Yet, if we take for granted that Jesus was God as confessed at Nicaea, there still remains the question, to what extent and in what manner of understanding and statement this truth is contained in the New Testament. A development from the Scriptures to Nicaea, at least in formulation and thought patterns, is recognized by all. Indeed, the council fathers at Nicaea were troubled over the fact that they could not answer the Arians in

purely biblical categories.[1] As contemporary scholars[2] have
so well shown, by the time of Nicaea there had been a
definite progression from a functional approach to Jesus
to an ontological approach. And so, it is perfectly legiti-
mate to push the question about the divinity of Jesus back
before Nicaea and to ask about the attitude of the New
Testament toward the problem.

However — and this is our second delimitation — the
New Testament attitude toward the divinity of Jesus is
much broader than the scope of this chapter. To treat
such a question, one would have to discuss all the important Christological titles, e.g., Messiah, Son of God,
Lord, Savior, etc., much in the manner of full-scale works
by V. Taylor, O. Cullmann, F. Hahn, R. H. Fuller, and
others. Such titles are an index of the way in which the
early Church confessed its understanding of what Jesus
meant for men. Even more important, one would have to
analyze the descriptions of Jesus' actions and miracles; his
attitudes toward the Temple, the Sabbath, and judgment;
his self-assurance in his proclamations and teaching; his
sinlessness; etc. If Jesus presented himself as one in whose
life God was active, he did so not primarily by the use of
titles or by clear statements about what he was, but rather
by the impact of his person and his life on those who
followed him. Thus, the material that would have to be
treated in discussing the divinity of Jesus in the New
Testament is very broad in range.

It is to only one small area of this material that we
confine this chapter, namely, the New Testament use of

[1] Athanasius, "Letters concerning the Decrees of the Council of
Nicaea," esp. chap. 5, nos. 19–21 (*Library of Nicene and Post-Nicene
Fathers*, Series 2, Vol. 4, 162–164).
[2] Cf. B. Lonergan, *De Deo trino* 1 (2nd ed.; Rome: Gregorian University, 1964) 104–112, 128–132, 153–154; J. C. Murray, *The Problem
of God* (New Haven: Yale University Press, 1964) pp. 40–41.

the term "God" (*theos*) for Jesus. Naturally, if the New Testament does use the term "God" in referring to Jesus, this is an important element in the larger question of the New Testament attitude toward the divinity of Jesus. But were we to discover that the New Testament never calls Jesus God, this would not necessarily mean that the New Testament authors did not think of Jesus as divine. There is much truth to Athanasius' contention[3] that the Nicene definition that Jesus was God and not a creature "collects the sense of Scripture," and thus, as we may deduce, is not dependent on any one statement of Scripture.

The limited nature of the topic we are treating does not diminish its importance, especially in ecumenical relations. In Protestant-Catholic dialogue a preference on the part of some Protestants for avoiding the phraseology "Jesus is God" is quite evident. The above-mentioned confession of the World Council of Churches provoked considerable criticism precisely because it stated that Jesus Christ was God. Some Catholics may suspect that neo-Arianism lies behind such criticism, and yet often it came from Christians who wholeheartedly accepted the truth implied in the phraseology. The uneasiness about calling Jesus God arises on several counts.

First, it has been argued that the statement "Jesus is God" is not a biblical formulation. It is to this problem that our chapter will be directly addressed. At the outset we may call attention to articles by such distinguished scholars as R. Bultmann[4] and V. Taylor,[5] who conclude

[3] *Op. cit.* 5, 21: "If the expressions are not in so many words in the Scriptures, yet they contain the sense of the Scriptures." Also 5, 20: "The Bishops . . . were compelled to collect the sense of the Scriptures."

[4] "The Christological Confession of the World Council of Churches," *Essays Philosophical and Theological* (New York: Scribners, 1955) pp. 273–290. The paper was given in 1951–1952.

[5] "Does the New Testament Call Jesus God?" *Expository Times* 73 (1961–1962) 116–118.

that the New Testament exercises great restraint in describing Jesus as God and who do not favor the designation. Other treatments by Oscar Cullmann[6] and A. W. Wainwright[7] seem to be slightly more positive in their evaluation of the evidence.

Second, it has been contended that this formula does not do justice to the fullness of Christ. Taylor says: "To describe Christ as God is to neglect the sense in which He is both less and more, man as well as God within the glory and limitations of His incarnation."[8] This fear that an exclusive emphasis on the divinity of Christ may lead to a failure to appreciate his humanity is quite realistic. Many believers unconsciously drift into a semidocetic understanding of Jesus which would exclude from his life such human factors as trial, fear, ignorance, and hesitation. However, the answer to this difficulty lies more in the direction of emphasizing the humanity of Jesus, rather than in questioning the validity of the formula "Jesus is God." Another aspect of the fear that this formula distorts the full picture of Jesus is the contention that the formula is open to a Sabellian interpretation that would reduce the Son to an aspect of God the Father. This danger seems less real in our times than the danger of semidocetism. If anything, the tendency in our times is to emphasize the Son at the expense of the Father and of the Holy Spirit.

Third, it has been contended that this formula objectivizes Jesus. Bultmann says: "The formula 'Christ is God' is false in every sense in which God is understood as an entity which can be objectivized, whether it is understood

[6] The Christology of the New Testament (London: S. C. M. Press, 1959) pp. 306–314.
[7] "The Confession 'Jesus is God' in the New Testament," Scottish Journal of Theology 10 (1957) 274–299.
[8] Art. cit., p. 118.

in an Arian or Nicene, an Orthodox or a Liberal sense. It is correct, if 'God' is understood as the event of God's acting."[9] He would avoid the danger by referring to Christ not as "God" but as "the Word of God." We may well wish to disengage ourselves from any exaggerated stress on the functional, for we maintain that it is meaningful and necessary to ask what Christ is in himself and not only what he is as far as we are concerned or for me personally.[10] Yet Bultmann's remarks do point up the danger of neglecting the soteriological implications of the formula "Jesus is God." Once again the answer to the danger would seem to lie in the proper explanation of the formula, rather than in its rejection. Nicaea certainly did not ignore the soteriological aspect, for in the one breath it described Jesus as "true God of true God . . . who for us men and our salvation . . . became man, suffered and rose."

Thus, it seems that the last two objections are centered primarily on the objectionable meaning that one can give to the formula "Jesus is God" and can be answered in terms of a corrective emphasis. We shall concentrate on the first objection and the scriptural justification for the formula. We shall discuss the important relevant texts under three headings: (I) texts that seem to imply that the title "God" was not used for Jesus; (II) texts where, by reason of textual variants or syntax, the use of "God" for Jesus is dubious; (III) texts where Jesus is clearly called

[9] *Art. cit.*, p. 287.

[10] Bultmann, *ibid.*, p. 280, maintains that a knowledge of the nature of Jesus without an accompanying knowledge of oneself is so inadequate that it can be compared with what Jas 2:19 says: "The devils also believe and tremble." On p. 284 Bultmann stresses that the true attitude of the New Testament is that God is to be encountered in Jesus. To what extent Bultmann's stress on "for me" relevance leads to an exaggerated functionalism has been debated; see G. Bornkamm, *Theologische Rundschau* 29 (1963) 127 ff.

God. We shall then evaluate the information that these texts give us about the frequency, antiquity, and origin of the use of "God" for Jesus.

I. TEXTS THAT SEEM TO IMPLY THAT THE TITLE "GOD" WAS NOT USED FOR JESUS

It seems best to begin with negative evidence which is often somewhat neglected in Catholic treatments of the subject. It is quite obvious that in the New Testament the term "God" is applied with overwhelming frequency to God the Father, i.e., to the God revealed in the Old Testament to whom Jesus prayed. The attitude toward Jesus in the early sermons of Acts is that Jesus was a man attested by God (2:22) and that God preached to Israel through Jesus (10:36). Throughout most of the New Testament there tends to be a distinction between God (= the Father) and Jesus. We may illustrate this by several texts.

1) Mk 10:18. In response to the man who addresses him as "good teacher," Jesus says: "Why do you call me good? No one is good but God alone." The crucial phrase (ei mē heis ho theos) may also be translated: ". . . but the one God." Lk 18:19 agrees with Mark but omits the article before theos. Mt 19:17 seems to reflect embarrassment at the thrust of the Marcan saying, for it reads: "Why do you ask me about what is good?" V. Taylor[11] lists a number of interpretations of this Marcan verse. A frequent patristic interpretation is that Jesus is trying to lead the man to a perception of his divinity, i.e., that Jesus is showing the man what he is really (and correctly)

[11] The Gospel according to St. Mark (London: Macmillan, 1953), pp. 426–427.

implying when he addresses Jesus as good. One cannot but feel that such an exegesis is motivated by an apologetic concern for protecting the doctrine of the divinity of Jesus. Other interpreters stress that Jesus is trying to direct attention away from himself to his Father. This is undoubtedly true, but it should not disguise the fact that this text strongly distinguishes between Jesus and God, and that a description which Jesus rejects is applicable to God. From this text one would never suspect that the evangelist thought of Jesus as God.[12]

2) Mk 15:34; Mt 27:46. As Jesus hangs on the cross, he cries out: "My God, my God, why have you forsaken me?" If either evangelist was accustomed to think or speak of Jesus as God, it is indeed strange that he would report a saying where Jesus is portrayed as addressing another as "my God." Of course, this argument is weakened by the fact that Jesus is citing Ps 22:1 and thus is using a conventional form of address. However, no such explanation is possible for the similar use of "my God" in Jn 20:17:[13]

[12] We shall treat all the Gospel passages on the level of what they reflect of the evangelists' mentality. Thus we shall not discuss two problems: (a) whether these are the *ipsissima verba* of Jesus; (b) what Jesus thought of himself in relation to divinity. We are exclusively concerned with whether the *New Testament authors* thought that "God" was a term applicable to Jesus.

[13] We cannot accept the contention that in this passage Jesus is making a careful (and theological) distinction between his own relationship to the Father and the relationship of his disciples to the Father, i.e., between natural sonship and the broader sonship gained through baptism. This passage must be interpreted against the background of Johannine theology: the ascension of which Jesus is speaking in 20:17 will lead to the giving of the Spirit (20:22; also 7:38–39), which will beget the disciples anew from above (3:3) and make them God's children (1:12). Thus Jesus' Father will now become the disciples' Father, and they will become Jesus' brothers (note that the message in 20:17 is to be relayed to his *brothers*). For an understanding of the construction in 20:17, see Ru 1:16: "Your people shall be my people; and your God, my God." Cf. F.-M. Catharinet, "Note sur un verset de l'évangile de Jean," *Mémorial J. Chaine* (Lyons: Facultés Catholiques, 1950) pp. 51–59.

"I am ascending to my Father and your Father, to my God and your God."

3) Eph 1:17: "The God of our Lord Jesus Christ, the Father of glory." (See also 2 Cor 1:3, 1 Pt 1:3.) In Eph 1:3 we hear of the "God and Father of our Lord Jesus Christ," but the abruptness of 1:17 makes an even stronger impression. Just as in the preceding Gospel examples wherein Jesus speaks of "my God," these examples from the Epistles make it difficult to think that the author designated Jesus as God.

4) There are several passages that by means of immediate juxtaposition seem to distinguish between the one God and Jesus Christ. We give a sampling:

> Jn 17:3: "Eternal life consists in this: that they know you, the only true God [ton monon alēthinon theon], and the one whom you sent, Jesus Christ."
>
> 1 Cor 8:6: "For us there is one God, the Father, from whom are all things and for whom we exist, and one Lord, Jesus Christ, through whom are all things and through whom we exist."
>
> Eph 4:4–6 distinguishes between ". . . one Spirit . . . one Lord . . . one God and Father of us all." In 1 Cor 12:4–6 a similar distinction is made: ". . . the same Spirit . . . the same Lord . . . the same God"; see also 2 Cor 13:14. Formulae distinguishing between the one God and Jesus Christ continued even after the New Testament period.[14]
>
> 1 Tim 2:5: "For there is one God, and there is one mediator between God and men, the man Christ Jesus."

Such passages closely associate Jesus the Lord and God the Father (and sometimes the Spirit as well); therefore, they are useful in discussing the New Testament attitude toward the divinity of Jesus and the New Testament roots of the later doctrine of the Trinity. However, for our

[14] Erik Peterson, *EIS THEOS* (Göttingen, 1926). For an example of a pertinent Jerash inscription, see BASOR 57 (1935) 8.

purposes they show that while Jesus was associated with God and was called the Lord or the mediator, there was a strong tendency to reserve the title "God" to the Father who is the one true God.

5) Tangentially related to our discussion are a number of texts which seem to state that Jesus is less than God or the Father. A full-scale exegesis of these texts would be germane to a paper discussing the divinity of Jesus in the New Testament;[15] it is not germane to our study here, for they do not directly involve the use of the title "God." Nevertheless, it is well at least to list them:

Jn 14:28: "The Father is greater than I." This is the third Johannine text we have mentioned in this section. It is important to note that there are Johannine passages that do not favor the application of the term "God" to Jesus. This will serve as a balance to the emphasis below that the fourth Gospel supplies us with clear examples of such an application.

Mk 13:32: "Of that day or that hour no one knows, not even the angels in heaven, nor the Son, but only the Father."

Phil 2:5–10: "Christ Jesus, who, though he was in the form (morphē) of God, did not count being equal with God a thing to be clung to, but emptied himself, taking the form of a servant. . . . Therefore God has highly exalted him and bestowed on him the name which is above every name . . . that every tongue should confess that Jesus is Lord, to the glory of God the Father."[16]

[15] Needless to say, for those who believe in Nicaea and Chalcedon, these texts will be explained in a way that will not deny the truth that from the first moment of his incarnation Jesus was true God and true man, and that the Son is equal to the Father.

[16] Attention is to be paid to the kenosis whereby Jesus emptied himself from a stage where he was in the form of God and equal to God to a stage where he took on the form of a servant. Also, it should be noted that in the exaltation at the end of this hymnal passage the name bestowed on Jesus is not "God" but "Lord." The "God" who exalted Jesus and bestowed the name upon him is God the Father.

1 Cor 15:24 speaks of the triumphant Christ of the Second Coming, who is to deliver the kingdom to God the Father In 15:28 Paul continues: "Then the Son himself will also be subjected to Him who put all things under him, that God may be everything to everyone." Some have suggested that Paul is speaking of the Son in his role as head of the Church, but in any case "God" is reserved as the title for Him to whom the Son is subjected.

II. TEXTS WHERE THE USE OF "GOD" FOR JESUS IS DUBIOUS

The doubts about these texts arise on two scores, namely, the presence of textual variants and problems of syntax.

A. Passages with textual variants[17]

1) Gal 2:20: "It is no longer I who live, but Christ who lives in me; and the life I now live in the flesh I live in faith, faith in the Son of God who loved me and gave himself for me."

The crucial words are en pistei zō tē tou huiou tou theou. Some important witnesses ((P[46], B, D*, G) read tou theou kai Christou instead of tou huiou tou theou. There are two ways to translate this variant: "faith in God and in Christ who loved me and gave himself for me," or "faith in the God and Christ, etc." Only in the second interpretation of this variant is "God" used as a title for Jesus. In general, critical editions of the Greek New Testament prefer the reading "Son of God" to the variant;

---

[17] We shall discuss only those which we think have some merit. We shall ignore, for instance, 1 Tim 3:16, where some of the later witnesses have God manifested in the flesh. The attestation for such a reading is not strong enough to warrant serious consideration.

but, in part, this is probably because the editors consider "Son of God" to be the less developed reading from a theological viewpoint and thus more original. The phrase *tou theou kai Christou* is never found elsewhere in the Pauline writings, and so is suspect. Thus, this text should not be counted among those passages which call Jesus God.

2) Acts 20:28: "The Holy Spirit has made you overseers to feed the church of God which he obtained with his own blood."

The crucial words are *tēn ekklēsian tou theou hēn periepoiēsato dia tou haimatos tou idiou.* There are two problems: one concerns the variant reading; the other concerns grammatical understanding.

In this instance "the church of God" is the best attested reading, with support in B, S, and the Vulgate. However, there is another reading, "the church of the Lord," which is supported by A, D, and some minor versions.[18] This second reading removes the possibility that Jesus is called God and is thus the less difficult reading — a fact which makes it suspect. However, an argument has been advanced for the second reading on the grounds that "the church of the Lord" is a much more unusual expression than "the church of God,"[19] and therefore some scribe may have tried to make the text conform to the usual expression, "the church of God." Yet the weight of the arguments favors "the church of God" as more original. One very plausible reason why some scribes may have

[18] The reading of the Byzantine text, "the church of the Lord and God," is obviously a scribal conflation.

[19] "The church of God" occurs eight times in the Pauline Epistles. "The church of the Lord" does not occur in the New Testament but does occur in the Septuagint as a translation of *qᵉhal YHWH*. We may mention that some interpreters see in this verse of Acts an echo of Ps 74:2: "Remember your congregation [or church] which you obtained of old."

changed "God" to "Lord" is that a reading which has God shedding blood seems to smack of Patripassianism.

If we accept "the church of God," then it is possible that the text is referring to Jesus as God, for the modifying clause "which he obtained with his own blood" would more appropriately be spoken of Jesus than of the Father. However, there is another possibility: perhaps *theos* refers to the Father and *idios* refers to the Son; thus, "the church of God (the Father) which He obtained with the blood of His own (Son)." Such a grammatical expert as Moulton favors this, and Hort once suggested that the Greek noun for Son may have been lost at the end of the verse. A recent and exhaustive Catholic treatment of this discourse in Acts[20] translates the verse in the way just proposed. And so, even if we read "the church of God," we are by no means certain that this verse calls Jesus God.

3) Jn 1:18: "No one has ever seen God; it is *God the only Son*, ever at the Father's side, who has revealed Him."

The textual witnesses do not agree on the italicized words; there are three major possibilities:

a) [*ho*] *monogenēs theos*, "God the only Son" or, as some would translate, "the only-begotten God."[21] This is supported by the evidence of the best Greek manuscripts, by the Syriac, by Irenaeus, Clement of Alexandria, and Origen. The fact that both of the recently discovered Bodmer papyri from ca. A.D. 200 have this reading gives it great weight. Some exegetes suspect that the reading is too highly developed theologically, but we shall see that elsewhere in John Jesus is clearly called God. One cannot

[20] J. Dupont, *Le discours de Milet* (Paris: Cerf, 1962) p. 159.

[21] However, *monogenēs* means "only, unique" (Latin *unicus*) and not "only-begotten"; the Vulgate's *unigenitus* represents anti-Arian apologetics on St. Jerome's part. For the evidence see D. Moody, *Journal of Biblical Literature* 72 (1953) 213–219.

maintain that this reading was introduced into copies of John as part of the anti-Arian polemic, for the Arians did not balk at giving such a title to Jesus. Perhaps the only real objection to the reading is the strangeness of the affirmation that God reveals God and that only God has seen God.

b) *monogenēs huios*, literally "the Son, the only one." This reading is supported by some early versions (Latin, Curetonian Syriac), by a good number of later Greek manuscripts, including A, by Athanasius, Chrysostom, and many of the Latin Fathers. In three of the other four uses of *monogenēs* in the Johannine writings,[22] it is combined with *huios*, and so the appearance of this combination here may be the reflection of a scribal tendency to conform.

c) *monogenēs*, "the only Son." This reading has the poorest attestation; it is found in Tatian, Origen (once), Epiphanius, and Cyril of Alexandria. Some scholars, e.g., Boismard, have favored it as the original reading, of which the above two readings would represent an expansion and clarification. However, the complete lack of attestation in the Greek copies of the Gospel makes it suspect. When one is dealing with patristic citations of the Gospel, one is never certain when, for the sake of brevity, the Fathers are citing only the essential words of a passage.

In our personal opinion, since the discovery of the Bodmer papyri, there is very good reason for accepting the first reading above as original — the reading which calls Jesus God.

B. *Passages where obscurity arises from syntax*

1) Col 2:2: ". . . that they may attain to all the riches of the fullness of understanding, unto the knowledge of the

[22] Jn 3:16, 18; 1 Jn 4:9.

mystery of God, Christ, in whom are hidden all the treas-
ures of wisdom and knowledge."

Several interpretations of the italicized phrase (tou theou
Christou) are possible:

a) "Christ" is in apposition to "God," or at least dependent on "God": "the knowledge of the mystery of the
God Christ." This interpretation calls Jesus God. There is
no article before "Christ," and so the two nouns may be
united. However, in the New Testament there is no other
instance of the formula "the God Christ."

b) The genitive "Christ" qualifies "God": "the knowledge of the mystery of the God of Christ." Grammatically
this offers no difficulty, and we saw above that Eph 1:17
speaks of "the God of our Lord Jesus Christ"; see also
Col 1:3.

c) "Christ" is the content of the mystery: "the knowledge of the mystery of God which is Christ." This
is actually the reading in D:[23] tou theou ho estin Christos
— a reading which reflects an early interpretation. Yet, the
reading in D points up the grammatical difficulty behind
this interpretation. If Paul had meant to say "the mystery
which is Christ," then he would normally have used the
Greek that is in Codex D, and not the tou theou Christou
which seems to be the original reading of the passage.[24]
The grammatical difficulty is not insuperable, however,
and an understanding of Paul's concept of "the mystery"[25]
would incline us to accept this interpretation.

[23] There are a number of variants in the textual witnesses. Their general
tenor is to distinguish between "God" and "Christ"; e.g., some add
"and" between the two words or qualify "God" as the Father. See T. K.
Abbott's commentary in the International Critical Commentary (New
York: Scribners, 1916) p. 240.

[24] For confirmatory examples of Pauline usage in such an instance, see
Col 1:24, 27; 1 Cor 3:11.

[25] See R. E. Brown, "The Semitic Background of the New Testament
Mysterion," Biblica 40 (1959) 72.

Be this as it may, the interpretations (b) and (c) are clearly preferable to (a), and therefore this text is not a good one to use in our discussion.

2) 2 Th 1:12: "So that the name of our Lord Jesus may be glorified in you, and you in him, according to the grace of our God and (the) Lord Jesus Christ."

The crucial Greek words are kata tēn charin tou theou hēmōn kai kyriou Iēsou Christou. There are two possible interpretations of the genitives: (a) "the grace of our God-and-Lord Jesus Christ"; (b) "the grace of our God and of the Lord Jesus Christ."

The first interpretation, which gives Jesus the title of "God," is favored by the absence in the Greek of an article before "Lord," giving the impression that the two genitives are bound together and governed by the one article which precedes "God." Yet, perhaps "Lord Jesus Christ" was so common a phrase that it would automatically be thought of as a separate entity and could be used without the article. The second interpretation is favored by the fact that hēmōn separates the two titles; but, as we shall see below in discussing 2 Pt 1:1, this is not a decisive argument. The most impressive argument for the second interpretation is that ho theos hēmōn, "our God," occurs four times in 1–2 Thessalonians as a title for God the Father; and on this analogy, in the passage at hand "our God" should be distinguished from "(the) Lord Jesus Christ."[26] Most commentators accept this distinction, and the latest and most comprehensive Catholic commentary[27] says that it must be

---

[26] Exactly the same problem exists for Jas 1:1, where James is described as "a servant of God and (the) Lord Jesus Christ" (theou kai kyriou Iēsou Christou doulos). However, in James there is no article before theou to suggest that the two nouns should be bound together as "God-and-Lord."

[27] B. Rigaux, Les épîtres aux Thessaloniciens (Paris: Gabalda, 1956) p. 643.

accepted. Therefore, this text cannot be offered as an example of the use of the title "God" for Jesus.

3) Tit 2:13: ". . . awaiting our blessed hope and the appearance of the glory of (the) great God and our Savior Jesus Christ."

The crucial Greek words are *epiphaneian tēs doxēs tou megalou theou kai sōtēros hēmōn Iēsou Christou*. Three interpretations are possible:

a) "the glory of the great god and of our Savior Jesus Christ." This interpretation, which clearly separates "the great God" and "our Savior Jesus Christ," is not really favored by the Greek, which binds together *theou kai sōtēros*. Once again it may be argued that the absence of an article before *sōtēros* is not too important, because "our Savior Jesus Christ" was so common a credal formula that it would automatically be thought of as a separate entity. However, the argument is less convincing here than it was above in the instance of 2 Th 1:12 where *hēmōn* broke up *theou . . . kai kyriou*. Moreover, the separation proposed in this interpretation of Tit 2:13 means that the author is speaking of a twofold glorious appearance, one of God and the other of the Savior Jesus Christ. There is no real evidence in the New Testament for such a double epiphany.

b) "the glory of our great God-and-Savior, which (glory) is Jesus Christ." This interpretation binds together "God" and "Savior" but applies the compound title to the Father. Jesus Christ is taken to represent the personification of the glory of God the Father, and grammatically *Iēsou Christou* is treated as a genitive in apposition with the genitive *doxēs*. The objection to this interpretation is the same as we faced in dealing with interpretation (c) of

Col 2:2, namely, that we would expect in the Greek an explanatory "which is." Otherwise, there is no real objection to the application of the title "Savior" to the Father, for other passages in Titus (1:3; 2:10; 3:4) speak of "God our Savior" (as contrasted with 1:4 and 3:6, which speak of "Jesus Christ our Savior"). Nor can one object to the idea that Jesus is the glory of the Father, for other New Testament passages[28] identify Jesus as the bearer of divine glory.

c) "the glory of our great God-and-Savior Jesus Christ." Here the compound title "God-and-Savior" is given to Jesus Christ. This is the most obvious meaning of the Greek. It implies that the passage is speaking only of one glorious epiphany, namely, of Jesus Christ; and this is in harmony with other references to the epiphany of Jesus Christ in the Pastoral Epistles (1 Tim 6:14–15; 2 Tim 4:1). That "Savior" is applied to Jesus Christ rather than to God the Father is suggested by the next verse in Titus (2:14), which speaks of the redemption wrought by Jesus. Some would rule out this interpretation which gives Jesus the title of "God" because elsewhere in the Pastorals (1 Tim 2:5; see above) a clear distinction is made between the one God (= the Father) and the man Jesus Christ. However, as we have noted, in the fourth Gospel there are passages which call Jesus God along with passages which distinguish between Jesus and the one true God.

It is very difficult to come to a definite decision. Careful scholars like Ezra Abbot and Joachim Jeremias have decided against interpretation (c). Yet Cullmann thinks that it is probable that Jesus is called God here, and the most complete Catholic commentary on the Pastorals[29] argues

[28] Jn 1:14; 12:41; 17:24; Heb 1:3.
[29] C. Spicq, *Les épîtres pastorales* (Paris: Gabalda, 1947) pp. 265–266.

strongly for this interpretation. Personally, we are inclined to recognize interpretation (c) as the probable meaning of the passage. It is unfortunate that no certainty can be reached here, for it seems that this passage is the one which shaped the confession of the World Council of Churches in "Jesus Christ as God and Savior."

> 4) 1 Jn 5:20: "And we know that the Son of God has come and has given us understanding to know Him who is true; and we are in Him who is true, in His Son Jesus Christ. *This is the true God* and eternal life."

In the first sentence of this passage it is quite obvious that "He who is true" (*ho alēthinos*) is God the Father; indeed, some textual witnesses[30] clarify the first "Him who is true" by adding "God," a combination that would be translated ". . . understanding to know *the true God*" (cf. Jn 17:3, cited above). This first sentence tells us that the Son has come and enabled men to know the Father, and the Christian abides in Father and Son.

The real problem concerns the opening of the second sentence in the passage:*houtos estin ho alēthinos theos*. To whom does the "this" (*houtos*) refer? C. H. Dodd[31] suggests that "this" is a general reference to the teaching of the Epistle. More often, however, it is seen as a reference to either "Jesus Christ" or to "Him who is true" in the preceding sentence. Grammar favors a reference to the nearest antecedent, and this would be "Jesus Christ." In this case Jesus Christ is called true God. Yet, since God the Father was referred to twice in the preceding sentence as *ho alēthinos*, one might suspect that the statement *houtos estin ho alēthinos theos* is really a reference to Him.

---

[30] Codex A, Vulg., Bohairic.
[31] *The Johannine Epistles* (London: Hodder and Stoughton, 1946) p. 140.

Certainly in Jn 17:3 *ho monos alēthinos theos* refers to God the Father and not to Jesus Christ.

Can we learn something from the second predicate in the sentence, i.e., "eternal life"? Twice in the fourth Gospel Jesus is called "the life" (11:25; 14:6), while the Father is never so called. Yet Jn 6:57 speaks of "the living Father" and makes it clear that the Father is the source of the Son's life. Thus it seems probable that in Johannine terminology either the Father or the Son could be designated as "life," even as they are both designated as "light" (1 Jn 1:5; Jn 8:12; note that it is the Epistle that calls the Father light, while the Gospel calls Jesus light). It may be, however, that the predicate "eternal life" does favor making Jesus Christ the subject of the sentence we are discussing, for only eight verses before (5:12) the author of the Epistle stated: "He who has the Son has life."

R. Schnackenburg,[32] who has given us the best commentary on 1 John, argues strongly from the logic of the context and the flow of the argument that "This is the true God" refers to Jesus Christ. The first sentence in 5:20 ends on the note that we Christians dwell in God the Father ("Him who is true") inasmuch as we dwell in His Son Jesus Christ. Why? Because Jesus is the true God and eternal life. Schnackenburg argues that the second sentence of 5:20 has meaning only if it refers to Jesus; it would be tautological if it referred to God the Father. His reasoning is persuasive, and thus there is a certain probability that 1 Jn 5:20 calls Jesus God — a usage not unusual in Johannine literature.

[32] *Die Johannesbriefe*, in *Herders theologischer Kommentar* (2nd ed.; Freiburg: Herder, 1963) p. 291. He cites Bultmann as recognizing that an addition by an editor who imitated the style of the epistle. Important scholars who deny a reference to Jesus include Harnack, Holtzmann, a reference to Jesus is more likely, but Bultmann regards the sentence as Brooke, and Windisch.

5) Rom 9:5: "Of their race [i.e., the Israelites] is the Christ according to the flesh God who is over all blessed forever."

The crucial Greek words are *ho Christos to kata sarka ho ōn epi pantōn theos eulogētos eis tous aiōnas*. The problem may be phrased in terms of various possible punctuations:

a) A full stop may be put after *sarka* ("flesh") as in Codex Ephraemi. The following words then become a separate sentence: "He who is God over all be [is] blessed forever"; or "He who is over all is God blessed forever." With either reading we have an independent doxology which seemingly refers to God the Father. Why Paul should stop here and introduce a doxology to the Father is not clear; for 9:1–5 concerns Christ, and one would expect praise of Christ, not of the Father. Moreover, the word order in the Greek offers considerable difficulty for this interpretation. In independent doxologies *eulogētos* ("blessed") as a predicate nominative normally comes first in the sentence;[33] here it is the sixth word in the sentence. The presence of the participle *ōn* is also awkward for this interpretation, for in either of the above readings it is superfluous. The construction *ho ōn* is normal only if there is an antecedent in the previous clause.[34]

b) A full stop may be put after *pantōn* ("all"), with a comma after *sarka*. Thus one obtains the reading: ". . . the Christ according to the flesh, who is over all. God be [is] blessed forever." This interpretation avoids the difficulty just mentioned about the presence of the participle *ōn*. In the independent doxology, however, *eulogētos* still does not have the normal first position in the sentence (it is now second), and the lack of contextual justification

33 See 2 Cor 1:3; Eph 1:3.
34 See 2 Cor 11:31; Rom 1:25.

for suddenly introducing a doxology to the Father remains a difficulty. On the whole, however, this interpretation seems preferable to (a).

c) A full stop may be put at the end, after aiōnas ("forever"), a comma after sarka. In this punctuation all the words after sarka are a relative clause modifying "Christ." Thus, ". . . the Christ according to the flesh, who is over all, God blessed forever." This interpretation would mean that Paul calls Jesus God. From a grammatical viewpoint this is clearly the best reading. Also, the contextual sequence is excellent; for, having spoken of Jesus' descent according to the flesh, Paul now emphasizes his position as God. The only real objection to this interpretation is that nowhere else does Paul speak of Jesus as God.[35]

This passage is a famous crux, and we cannot hope to reach a decision that will be accepted by all. Distinguished scholars are aligned on both sides. Among those who think that Rom 9:5 applies the title "God" to Jesus are Sanday and Headlam, G. Findlay, Boylan, Nygren, Lagrange, and O. Michel. Among those who think that the reference is to the Father are H. Meyer, Dodd, Bultmann, J. Knox, Barrett, and Taylor. Personally, we are inclined to accept

[35] Already in this section we have rejected such texts as Gal 2:20; 1 Tim 3:16 (n. 17 above); Col 2:2; 2 Th 1:12; in the previous section we pointed out a number of Pauline texts which would seem to indicate that Paul did not refer to Jesus as God. In our opinion, besides Rom 9:5, the only Pauline text that has real plausibility as an instance of Jesus' being called God is Tit 2:13. But this is in the Pastoral Epistles, which many scholars regard as deutero-Pauline. Nevertheless, it may be argued that, whether or not they were written by Paul, the Pastorals are a homogeneous development of Pauline usage; thus the usage in Tit 2:13 may be interpreted as a continuation of Paul's own way of speaking already instanced in Rom 9:5. — We should caution that an argument based on Paul's usage or nonusage of "God" for Jesus is different from the claim that Paul was so imbued with Jewish monotheism that he could not have thought of Jesus as God. Such a claim assumes that Paul could find no way of reconciling two truths. Wainwright, art. cit., p. 276, rightly criticizes this circular reasoning.

the grammatical evidence in favor of interpretation (c), but at most one may claim a certain probability that this passage refers to Jesus as God.

> 6) 2 Pt 1:1: "To those who have obtained a faith of equal standing with ours in the righteousness of our God and Savior Jesus Christ."

The crucial Greek words are en dikaiosynē tou theou hēmōn kai sōtēros Iēsou Christou. The grammatical problem is the same as we saw in 2 Th 1:12, where we favored the interpretation "the grace of our God and of the Lord Jesus Christ," a reading that distinguished between God (the Father) and Jesus Christ. If one were to follow the analogy, one would translate here "the righteousness of our God and of the Savior Jesus Christ." However, 2 Peter offers a parallel construction which enables us to decide that the author very probably intended both titles, "God" and "Savior," to be applied to Jesus Christ. In 2 Pt 1:11 we hear of "the eternal kingdom of our Lord-and-Savior Jesus Christ" (basileian tou kyriou hēmōn kai sōtēros Iēsou Christou). Here there can be no reasonable doubt that "Lord" and "Savior" constitute a compound title for Jesus, and it seems logical to interpret 1:1 on the analogy of 1:11.[36] This passage could almost be classified in the next section of our article under texts which clearly call Jesus God.

In the second main section, we have considered nine texts where the use of "God" for Jesus is dubious. In the first subsection (passages with textual variants) we rejected Gal 2:20 and Acts 20:28 as too uncertain, but recognized Jn 1:18 as a very probable instance where Jesus is called

---

[36] When 2 Pt 1:2 does distinguish between God (the Father) and Jesus, another word order is used: ". . . in the knowledge of God and of Jesus our Lord" (en epignōsei tou theou kai Iēsou tou kyriou hēmōn).

God. In the second subsection (passages where obscurity arises from syntax) we rejected Col 2:2 and 2 Th 1:12, but recognized in Tit 2:13; 1 Jn 5:20; Rom 9:5; and 2 Pt 1:1 instances in which in ascending order there is increasing probability that Jesus is called God. Thus, five of the nine instances must be taken seriously in our discussion. A methodological note is in order here. Often these five examples are rejected by scholars, despite the grammatical arguments in their favor, on the grounds that the use of "God" for Jesus is rare in the New Testament and therefore always to be considered improbable.[37] However, is not the rarity of the usage to some extent dependent on the rejection of these examples? If these five instances are joined to the three we shall cite in the next section, then the usage is not so rare.

III. TEXTS WHERE JESUS IS CLEARLY CALLED GOD

There are a number of passages in the New Testament which *imply* that Jesus is divine,[38] but we shall confine our attention to three passages that explicitly use *theos* of Jesus.

1) Heb 1:8-9: The author says that God has spoken of Jesus His Son the words of Ps 45: 6-7:

8 "Your throne, O *God*, is forever and ever . . . and the righteous scepter is the scepter of your [his] kingdom.

[37] Wainwright, art. cit., p. 277, makes two points worth repeating. First, "Many critics have chosen a less natural translation of the Greek because they believe it was psychologically impossible for the writer to have said that Christ was God." Second, the argument from inconsistency in usage (i.e., elsewhere the writer does not call Jesus God) must be used with care, for we are not certain that the writer saw an inconsistency in only occasionally using a title.

[38] Besides those cited in n. 47 below, we may mention Jn 10:30, "I and the Father are one"; 14:9, "He who has seen me has seen the Father"; the absolute use of egō eimi ("I AM") in Jn 8:24, 28, 58; 13:19.

⁹ You have loved justice and hated iniquity; therefore,
O God, your God has anointed you with the oil of
gladness. . . ."

The psalm is cited according to the Septuagint.³⁹ The
first question we must ask is whether *ho theos* in v. 8 is a
nominative or a vocative. A few scholars, including West-
cott, have taken it as a nominative and have suggested the
interpretation: "God is your throne for ever and ever."
This is most unlikely. In the preceding verse of the psalm
in the Septuagint we read: "Your weapons, O Mighty
One, are sharpened"; the law of parallelism would indicate
that the next verse should read: "Your throne, O God, is
for ever and ever." Moreover, the parallelism from the
very next line in the psalm, cited in v. 8 ("and the righteous scepter is . . ."), suggests that "throne" and not
"God" is the subject of the line under consideration.
There can be little doubt, then, that the reading of v. 8
which we have proposed is the correct one. Cullmann⁴⁰
assures us that "Hebrews unequivocally applies the title
'God' to Jesus," and we believe that this is a true estimate
of the evidence of v. 8.

V. Taylor⁴¹ admits that in v. 8 the expression "O God"

³⁹ Actually, the Septuagint reading is a misunderstanding of the Maso-
retic Text, but this is a problem in psalm exegesis and does not affect
the meaning of the citation in Hebrews.

⁴⁰ *Op. cit.*, p. 310. Perhaps there is also a reference to Jesus as God
in v. 9. The translation of v. 9 we have given follows C. Spicq, *L'épître
aux Hébreux* 2 (Paris: Gabalda, 1953) 19 ff., in taking the first *ho theos*
as a vocative and the second *ho theos* (*sou*) as the subject of the verb,
thus: "O God [= Jesus], your God [= the Father] has anointed you."
However, it is possible to take the first *ho theos* as the subject of the verb
and the second *ho theos* (*sou*) as an appositive, thus: "God, your God,
has anointed you." In the latter interpretation "God, your God" is the
Father.

⁴¹ *Art. cit.*, p. 117. The type of argument Taylor advances is not im-
plausible. For instance, Mt 1:23 cites Is 7:14 in relation to the birth
of Jesus: ". . . his name shall be called Emmanuel (which means 'God
with us')." We cannot be certain that, because he used this citation, the
evangelist took "God with us" literally and meant to call Jesus God.

is a vocative spoken of Jesus, but he says that the author of Hebrews was merely citing the psalm and using its terminology without any deliberate intention of suggesting that Jesus is God. It is true that the main point of citing the psalm was to contrast the Son with the angels and to show that the Son enjoys eternal domination, while the angels are but servants. Therefore, in the citation no major point was being made of the fact that the Son can be addressed as God. Yet we cannot presume that the author did not notice that his citation had this effect. We can say, at least, that the author saw nothing wrong in this address, and we can call upon the similar situation in Heb 1:10, where the application to the Son of Ps 102:25–27 has the effect of addressing Jesus as Lord. Of course, we have no way of knowing what the "O God" of the psalm meant to the author of Hebrews when he applied it to Jesus. Ps 45 is a royal psalm; and on the analogy of the "Mighty God" of Is 9:6,[42] "God" may have been looked on simply as a royal title and hence applicable to Jesus as the Davidic Messiah.

   2) Jn 1:1: "In the beginning was the Word;
          and the Word was in God's presence,
          and the Word was God."

The crucial Greek words of the second and third lines are *kai ho logos ēn pros ton theon kai theos ēn ho logos*. The debate about the third line centers on the fact that *theos* is used without an article. Clearly, in the second line *ho theos* refers to God the Father, but in predicating *theos* without the article *ho* of the Word in the third line is the

---

[42] We do not mean to imply that Isaiah necessarily intended *'ēl gibbōr* to mean "Mighty God," but that by New Testament times this may have been the understanding of Is 9:6. In Jn 10:34 we have an instance where the Old Testament reference to the judges as "gods" is interpreted as a reference to divinity.

author trying to suggest that the Word is somewhat less than the Father (see Jn 14:28)?[43]

Some explain the usage with the simple grammatical rule that predicate nouns generally lack the article. However, while *theos* is most probably the predicate, such a rule does not necessarily hold for a statement of identity (e.g., the "I am . . ." formulae in Jn 11:25 and 14:6 are followed by predicate nouns which have an article).

To preserve the nuance of the anarthrous *theos*, some (e.g., Moffatt) would translate: "The Word was divine." But this is too weak. After all, there is in Greek an adjective for "divine" (*theios*) which the author did not choose to use.[44] The *New English Bible* paraphrases the line: "What God was, the Word was." This is certainly better than "divine," but loses the terseness of the Prologue's style. Perhaps the best explanation of why the author of the Prologue chose to use *theos* without the article to refer to the Word is that he desired to keep the word distinct from the Father (*ho theos*).

Several factors suggest that we should not attach too

[43] The Catholic exegete S. de Ausejo, "¿Es un himno a Cristo el prólogo de San Juan?" *Estudios bíblicos* 15 (1956) 223–277, 381–427, has made the suggestion that throughout the Prologue "the Word" means the Word-become-flesh and that the whole hymn refers to Jesus Christ in the strict sense (i.e., in the language of later theology, to the incarnate rather than to the preincarnate Second Person). The fact that Jn 1:1 is set in the beginning before creation does not militate against this, for other New Testament hymns speak of Jesus Christ even when they have verses which are seemingly in a preincarnational setting (Phil 2:5–7 speaks of Christ Jesus who emptied himself, taking the form of a servant; Eph 1:3–4 says that God chose us in Christ before the foundation of the world). If de Ausejo's suggestion is true, there could be some justification in seeing in the anarthrous *theos* something more humble than the *ho theos* used of the Father, along the lines of Jn 14:28. The hymn of Phil 2:5–7 says that the incarnate Jesus had humbled himself to the form of a servant.

[44] E. Haenchen, "Probleme des johanneischen 'Prologs,'" *Zeitschrift für Theologie und Kirche* 60 (1963) 313 n. 38, argues that even if the author meant to say "divine," he would not have used such an adjective, for it smacks of high literary style. This objection is too subjective.

much theological importance to the lack of the article. This first verse of the Prologue forms an inclusion with the last line of the Prologue, and there (1:18; see above) we hear of "God the only Son" ([ho] monogenēs theos). Moreover, as the beginning of the Gospel, the first verse of the Prologue also forms an inclusion with the (original) end of the Gospel, where in 20:28 Thomas calls Jesus "My Lord and my God."[45] Neither of the passages involved in these inclusions would suggest that in Johannine thought Jesus was theos but less than ho theos. To a certain extent, calling Jesus God represents for the fourth Gospel a positive answer to the charges made against Jesus that he was arrogantly making himself God (Jn 10:33; 5:18). The Roman author Pliny the Younger[46] describes the Christians of Asia Minor as singing hymns to Christ as to a God. The Prologue, a hymn of the Johannine community at Ephesus, fits this description, as do the similar Pauline hymns in Philippians and Colossians.[47]

It may be well to re-emphasize what we stated at the beginning of this article, namely, that the Prologue's hymnic confession "The Word was God" does not have the same ideological content found in Nicaea's confession that the Son was "true God of true God." A different problematic and a long philosophical development separate the two.

[45] We presuppose a critical approach to the composition of the fourth Gospel, e.g., the recognition that chap. 21 is a late addition to the Gospel; the Prologue is an independent hymn that was subsequently adapted to introduce the Gospel.

[46] Ep. 10, 96, 7.

[47] See D. M. Stanley, "Carmenque Christo quasi Deo dicere," Catholic Biblical Quarterly 20 (1958) 173–191. Phil 2:6–7 says that before he took on the form of a servant, Jesus was in the form of God; Col 1:19 says that in the Son all the fullness of God was pleased to dwell; Col 1:15 calls him the image of the invisible God. It is generally admitted today that in these instances Paul is citing hymns. Colossae is in Asia Minor; many think that Philippians was written from Ephesus.

3) Jn 20:28: On the Sunday evening one week after Easter Jesus appears to Thomas and the other disciples, and Thomas confesses him as "My Lord and my God."

This is the clearest example in the New Testament of the use of "God" for Jesus,[48] for the contention of Theodore of Mopsuestia that Thomas was uttering an exclamation of thanks to the Father finds few proponents today. Here Jesus is addressed as God (*ho theos mou*), with the articular nominative serving as a vocative. The scene is designed to serve as a climax to the Gospel: as the resurrected Jesus stands before the disciples, one of their number at last gives expression to an adequate faith in Jesus. He does this by applying to Jesus the Greek equivalent of two terms applied to the God of the Old Testament. The best example of the Old Testament usage is in Ps 35:23, where the psalmist cries out: "My God and my Lord." It may well be that the Christian use of such a confessional formula was catalyzed by Domitian's claim to the title *dominus et deus noster*.

IV. EVALUATION OF THE EVIDENCE

The question that forms the title of this chapter must be answered in the affirmative. In three clear instances and in five instances that have a certain probability[49] Jesus is

[48] Bultmann, art. cit., p. 276: "The only passage in which Jesus is undoubtedly designated or, more exactly, addressed as God." This is an exaggeration, however, for it does not give proper emphasis to the probabilities or, indeed, certainties that Heb 1:8; 1 Jn 5:20; and 2 Pt 1:1 refer to Jesus as God. Moreover, it draws more attention than is warranted to the fact that theos is used with an article in Jn 20:28 and without an article in Jn 1:1. After all, kyrios as a title for Jesus sometimes has the article and sometimes does not (see discussion of 2 Th 1:12 above). C. K. Barrett, *The Gospel According to John* (London: SPCK Press, 1956) p. 477, warns apropos of Jn 20:28: "The difference between the present verse and 1:1 (where theos is anarthrous) cannot be pressed."

[49] The neglect of these five instances is what, in our opinion, makes Taylor's and Bultmann's treatment of the question too pessimistic; e.g.,

called God in the New Testament. The use of *theos* of Jesus which is attested in the early second century was a continuation of a usage which had begun in New Testament times. Really, there is no reason to be surprised at this. "Jesus is Lord" was evidently a popular confessional formula in New Testament times, and in this formula Christians gave Jesus the title *kyrios* which was the standard Septuagint translation for YHWH.[50] If Jesus could be given this title, why could he not be called *theos*, which the Septuagint often used to translate *'elōhîm?* The two Hebrew terms had become relatively interchangeable, and indeed YHWH was the more sacred term.

This does not mean that we can take a naïve view about the development that took place in the New Testament usage of "God" for Jesus (nor, for that matter, in the gradual development in the understanding of Jesus' divinity[51]). The eight instances with which we are concerned

---

Bultmann, *art. cit.,* 276: "It is only with the Apostolic Fathers that free, unambiguous reference to Jesus Christ as 'our God' begins." As we have insisted, the textual or grammatical probabilities favor the interpretation that these five passages call Jesus God. In one or the other instance the interpretation may be wrong, but simply to write off all five as unconvincing and therefore unimportant for the discussion is not good method. It would be foolish to develop a theory about the New Testament use of "God" for Jesus that would depend for a key point on one of these five texts, but it would be just as foolish to develop a theory that would be invalid if Jesus is really called God in several of these instances. In all that follows, we intend to take these five instances seriously.

[50] We do not raise the disputed question of the origins (Palestinian or Hellenistic) of the New Testament usage of *kyrios,* nor do we assume that every time *kyrios* appears it is used consciously as a translation of YHWH. But we do maintain that in general the New Testament authors were aware that Jesus was being given a title which in the Septuagint referred to the God of Israel.

[51] The 1964 Instruction of the Pontifical Biblical Commission, *The Historical Truth of the Gospels,* in section VIII recognizes that only after Jesus rose from the dead was his divinity clearly perceived. We need not think that this perception was the work of a moment; it took a long time for men to come to understand the mystery of Jesus and to give it formulation. The Arian dispute shows this clearly.

are found in these New Testament writings: Romans, Hebrews, Titus, John, 1 John, and 2 Peter. Let us see what
this means in terms of chronology.

Jesus is never called God in the Synoptic Gospels, and
a passage like Mk 10:18 would seem to preclude the possibility that Jesus used the title of himself. Even the fourth
Gospel never portrays Jesus as saying specifically that he
is God.[52] The sermons which Acts attributes to the beginning of the Christian mission do not speak of Jesus as God.
Thus, there is no reason to think that Jesus was called God
in the earliest layers of New Testament tradition. This
negative conclusion is substantiated by the fact that Paul
does not use the title in any epistle written before 58. The
first likely occurrence of the usage of "God" for Jesus is in
Rom 9:5; if we could be certain of the grammar of this
passage, we could thus date the usage to the late 50's.

Chronologically, Heb 1:8–9 and Tit 2:13 would be the
next examples, although the uncertainty of the date of
composition of these epistles creates a problem. Hebrews
cannot be dated much before the fall of Jerusalem, and
many would place it even later. The date of Titus depends
on the acceptance or rejection of the Pauline authorship of

[52] More than the other Gospels, John brings the "God problem" to the
fore in the ministry of Jesus (5:18; 7:58–59; 10:30–33); this is part of the
Johannine technique of spelling out the challenge that Jesus brings to
men, and of making explicit what was implicit in Jesus' ministry. Yet
John does show a certain caution about anachronism and so even in
10:33 ff. Jesus does not give a clear affirmation to the charge of the
Jews that he is making himself God. These disputes must be understood
against the background of the evangelist's own time and the attacks
of the Synagogue of the 80's and 90's on Christian claims about Jesus. —
Jn 20:28 portrays Jesus being confessed as God one week after the
resurrection. Without necessarily questioning the Johannine tradition of
an appearance to Thomas, one who would evaluate the scene critically
would suspect that a confessional formula of the evangelist's own time
has been used to vocalize the apostle's belief in the resurrected Jesus.
Were the title "God" used for Jesus so soon after the resurrection, one
could not explain the absence of this title in Christian confessions before
the 60's. See n. 63 below.

the Pastorals — scholarly views range from the middle 60's to the end of the century.[53] The Johannine writings offer us the most frequent examples of the use of the title (three in John; one in 1 John), and these writings are generally dated in the 90's. The common opinion of recent exegetes, Catholics included, is that 2 Peter is one of the latest New Testament works.

If we date New Testament times from 30 to 100, quite clearly the use of "God" for Jesus belongs to the second half of the period[54] and becomes frequent only toward the end of the period. This judgment is confirmed by the evidence of the earliest extrabiblical Christian works.[55] At the beginning of the second century Ignatius freely speaks of Jesus as God. In *Ephesians* 18, 2 he says: "Our God, Jesus the Christ, was conceived by Mary"; in 19, 3 he says: "God was manifest as man." In *Smyrnaeans* 1, 1 Ignatius begins by giving glory to "Jesus Christ, the God who has thus given you wisdom."[56] We have already cited Pliny's

[53] Most Catholic scholars will incline toward Pauline authorship, at least in that broad sense of authorship which governs the attribution of biblical books. In any case, the Pastoral Epistles are intimately associated with Paul's thought and activity; and whether or not Paul is the author, they should not be dated too long after Paul's ministry.

[54] Of course, there is a danger in judging usage from occurrence in the New Testament. New Testament occurrence does not create a usage but testifies to a usage already extant. None of the passages we have cited gives any evidence of innovating, and indeed a passage like Heb 1:8–9 seems to call on an already traditional use of the psalm. Yet frequency of New Testament occurrence in a question such as we are dealing with is probably a good index of actual usage. Nor can we forget that the passages cited under the first main section above show that Jesus was not spoken of as God in many New Testament works. Any theory which holds that from the very beginning Jesus was called God, but that by accident this usage does not occur till late in the New Testament, is a theory that does not explain the facts.

[55] Some authors cite *Didache* 10, 6, where "Hosanna to the God of David" is addressed to Jesus. However, J.-P. Audet, in his exhaustive commentary on the *Didache* (Paris: Gabalda, 1958) pp. 62–67, argues strongly for the originality of the reading "Hosanna to the *house* of David."

[56] See also *Trallians* 7, 1; *Romans* 7, 3. The reference in *Ephesians* 1,

testimony at the turn of the century that the Christians of Asia Minor sang hymns to Christ as to a God. By mid-second century, the so-called 2 Clement (1, 1) can state: "Brethren, we must think of Jesus Christ as of God."

The geographical spread of the usage is also worth noting. If Rom 9:5 is accepted, then Paul, writing from Greece, betrays no hesitation about the acceptability of the usage to his Roman audience. (Yet Mark, traditionally accepted as the Gospel of Rome, written in the 60's, does not hesitate to report a saying of Jesus in which he refuses to be called God: see Mk 10:18 above.) If Titus is accepted as a genuinely Pauline epistle, it was probably written from Macedonia to Titus in Crete. The place of the composition of Hebrews is not known: Alexandria is a prominent candidate, and either Palestine or Rome is thought to be the destination. The Johannine works are associated with Ephesus in Asia Minor. Ignatius, from Antioch,[57] seems free to use "God" of Jesus when writing both to Asia Minor and to Rome. Pliny's statement reflects the Christian practice in Bithynia in Asia Minor. Thus, the usage seems to be attested in the great Christian centers of the New Testament world, and there is no evidence to support a claim that in the late first century the custom of calling Jesus God was confined to a small area or faction within the Christian world.

Is this usage a Hellenistic contribution to the theological vocabulary of Christianity? Since we have no evidence

---

1 to "God's blood" is reminiscent of one of the above-cited interpretations of Acts 20:28: "the church of God which he obtained with his own blood."

[57] The Gospel of Matthew is often associated with the church of Syria-Palestine. The fact that Mt 19:17 modifies Mk 10:18 and Jesus' rejection of the title of God (above, first main section) may be a witness that the custom of calling Jesus God was alive in this church long before Ignatius' time.

that Jesus was called God in the Jerusalem or Palestinian communities of the first two decades of Christianity, the prima-facie evidence might suggest Hellenistic origins. This is supported by the fact that in two New Testament passages "God" is intimately joined to "Savior" as a title for Jesus (Tit 2:13; 2 Pt 1:1), and "Savior" is to some extent a Hellenistic title. However, there is other evidence to suggest that the usage had its roots in the Old Testament; and so, if the usage is non-Palestinian, it may have arisen among converts from Diaspora Judaism. As we saw, Heb 1:8–9 is a citation of Ps 45. The confession of Thomas in Jn 20:28 echoes an Old Testament formula (although, as we pointed out, one cannot exclude the possibility of an anti-Domitian apologetic). The background for Jn 1:1 is the opening of Genesis, and the concept of the Word reflects Old Testament themes of the creative word of God and personified Wisdom. Perhaps the best we can do from the state of the evidence is to leave open the question of the background of the custom of calling Jesus God.

The slow development of the usage of the title "God" for Jesus requires explanation. Not only is there the factor that Jesus is not called God in the earlier strata of New Testament material, but also there are passages cited in the first series of texts above, that by implication reserve the title "God" for the Father. Moreover, even in the New Testament works that speak of Jesus as God, there are also passages that seem to militate against such a usage — a study of these texts will show that this is true of the Pastorals and the Johannine literature. The most plausible explanation is that in the earliest stage of Christianity the Old Testament heritage dominated the use of the title "God"; hence "God" was a title too narrow to be applied to Jesus. It referred strictly to the Father of Jesus, to the

God to whom he prayed. Gradually (in the 50's and 60's?), in the development of Christian thought "God" was understood to be a broader term.[58] It was seen that God had revealed so much of Himself in Jesus that "God" had to be able to include both Father and Son.[59] The late Pauline works seem to fall precisely in this stage of development.[60] If Rom 9:5 calls Jesus God, it is an isolated instance within the larger corpus of the main Pauline works, which think of Jesus as Lord and of the Father as God. By the time of the Pastorals, however, Jesus is well known as God-and-Savior. The Johannine works come from the final years of the century, when the usage is common. Yet some of the material that has gone into the fourth Gospel is traditional material about Jesus which has been handed down from a much earlier period. Therefore, there are passages in John (14:28; 17:3; 20:17) that reflect an earlier mentality. We can only sketch the broad lines of such a development, but we can be reasonably confident that these lines are true.

We can, perhaps, go further and suggest the ambiance of this development. We think that the usage of calling Jesus God was a liturgical usage and had its origin in the worship and prayers of the Christian community. A priori,

[58] Probably there was a similar development in the use of "Lord" (kyrios) wherever it was thought of as a translation of YHWH. Yet kyrios was applied to Jesus much more quickly than theos. Was the more obvious danger of a polytheistic conception in the use of theos a retarding factor? Did the fact that kyrios had a range of meaning below the divine ("lord," "master") favor the use of that term? See n. 50 above.

[59] We omit from our discussion the problem of the Holy Spirit, a problem complicated by uncertainty as to when the New Testament authors began to think of the Spirit (Greek pneuma, neuter) as a personal factor.

[60] Here we must be acutely aware of the limits imposed on our research by the very nature of the Pauline writings. The fact that Jesus is (presumably) called God in Romans, but not in Thessalonians, may be accidental. (Yet see n. 54 above.) Therefore we can speak only of what seems to be true from the evidence available.

this is not unlikely. Bultmann[61] has long maintained that the title "Lord" was given to Jesus in the Hellenistic communities as they recognized him as the deity present in the act of worship. Without committing ourselves to this theory and its implications, we do recognize the liturgical setting of some instances of the confession of Jesus as Lord, and therefore we might anticipate a similar setting for the confession of Jesus as God.

Of the eight instances of the latter confession, the majority are clearly to be situated in a background of worship and liturgy. Four are doxologies (Tit 2:13; 1 Jn 5:20; Rom 9:5; 2 Pt 1:1), and it is well accepted that many of the doxologies in the epistolary literature of the New Testament echo doxologies known and used by the respective communities in their public prayer. Heb 1:8–9 cites a psalm that was applied to Jesus, and we know the custom of singing psalms in Christian celebrations (1 Cor 14:26; Eph 5:19). Certainly this would include Old Testament psalms that were thought to be particularly adaptable to Jesus. Thus, it is not too adventurous of Wainwright to suggest that the author of Hebrews was calling on psalms that his readers sang in their liturgy and was reminding them of how these psalms voiced the glory of Jesus. The Prologue of John, which twice calls Jesus God, was originally a hymn, and we have already recalled Pliny's dictum about the Christians singing hymns to Christ as to a God.[62]

Perhaps, at first glance, Jn 20:28 seems an exception to the rule, for the confession of Thomas is given a historical rather than a liturgical setting. Yet even here the scene is carefully placed on a *Sunday*, when the disciples of Jesus are gathered together. Moreover, it is a very plausible sug-

[61] E.g., art. cit., p. 277.
[62] Also see n. 47 above.

gestion that the words in which Thomas confesses Jesus, "My Lord and my God," represent a confessional formula known in the Church of the evangelist's time.[63] In this case it is not unlikely that the confession is a baptismal or liturgical formula along the lines of "Jesus is Lord."

This theory of the liturgical origins of the usage of the title "God" for Jesus in New Testament times has some very important implications concerning the meaning of this title, and, indeed, goes a long way toward answering some of the objections against calling Jesus God, such as those mentioned at the beginning of the article. For instance, it was objected that calling Jesus God neglects the limits of the incarnation. But this objection is not applicable to the New Testament usage, for there the title "God" is not directly given to the Jesus of the ministry. In the Johannine writings it is the pre-existent Word (1:1) or the Son in the Father's presence (1:18) or the resurrected Jesus (20:28) who is hailed as God. The doxologies confess as God the triumphant Jesus; Heb 1:8–9 is directed to Jesus whose throne is forever. Thus, in the New Testament there is no obvious conflict between the passages that call Jesus God and the passages that seem to picture the incarnate Jesus as less than God or the Father.[64] The problem of how during his lifetime Jesus could be both God and man is presented in the New Testament, not by the use of the title "God," but by some of the later strata of

---

[63] The 1964 Instruction of the Pontifical Biblical Commission, *The Historical Truth of the Gospels*, has recognized that the evangelists do not always give us the *ipsissima verba* from the time of Jesus, and that they have explicated the material handed down by apostolic tradition. Barrett, *op. cit.*, p. 477, concurs on the liturgical coloring of the passage under discussion.

[64] See the passages cited in the first main section above, nos. 1 and 5. The only passage that really offers a difficulty in this connection is 1 Cor 15:24, for here Paul speaks of the triumphant Son as subject to the Father. This text needs a good deal more study in the light of Nicene Christology.

Gospel material which bring Jesus' divinity to the fore even before the resurrection.[65] Ignatius of Antioch does use the title "God" of Jesus during his human career. This may be the inevitable (and true) development of the New Testament usage of calling the preincarnational and the resurrected Jesus God; but from the evidence we have, it is a post-New Testament development.

The liturgical ambiance of the New Testament usage of "God" for Jesus also answers the objection that this title is too much of an essential definition, which objectifies Jesus and is untrue to the soteriological interest of the New Testament. As far as we can see, no one of the instances we have discussed attempts to define Jesus essentially.[66] The acclamation of Jesus as God is a response of prayer and worship to the God who has revealed Himself to men in Jesus. Jn 1:18 speaks of God the only Son who has revealed the Father: Jn 1:1 tells us that God's Word is God. The confession of Jesus as God is a recognition by believing subjects of the sovereignty and lordship of divine rule in, through, and by Jesus: thus, Thomas' "My Lord and my God" (Jn 20:28), and Romans' (9:5) "God who is over all," and Hebrews' (1:8) "Your throne, O God, is for ever and ever." How could the confession of Jesus as God be more soteriological than when Jesus is called "our

[65] E.g., the infancy narratives, which show the child of Bethlehem to have been conceived by no human father; and the fourth Gospel, in which the Jesus of the ministry makes divine claims.

[66] Even in Jn 1:1 the approach is largely functional. There are no speculations about how the Word is related to God the Father; and the very designation "the Word" implies a speaking to an audience. The fact that 1:1 is set "in the beginning" relates the Word to creation. Nevertheless, it is true to say that passages like Jn 1:1 would be destined soon and inevitably to raise questions of more than a functional nature. E. Käsemann, *Jesu letzter Wille nach Johannes 17* (Tübingen: Mohr, 1966), p. 47, says of this fourth Gospel: "The question of the nature of Christ is now thematically discussed, still in the framework of soteriology of course, but with an importance and isolation that can no longer be accounted for in terms of exclusively soteriological interest."

God-and-Savior" (2 Pt 1:1; Tit 2:13)? If there is validity in Bultmann's concern that belief in Jesus must have reference for me, then he can have no objection to what 1 Jn 5:20 says of Jesus Christ: "This is the true God *and eternal life*."

Thus, even though we have seen that there is a solid biblical precedent for calling Jesus God, we must be cautious to evaluate this usage in terms of the New Testament ambiance. Our firm adherence to the later theological and ontological developments in the meaning of the formula "Jesus is God" must not cause us to overvalue or undervalue the New Testament confession.

CHAPTER TWO

How Much Did Jesus Know?

Writing this chapter[1] has not been an entirely pleasant task. Although today we are not much given to sentiment, there is an almost instinctive distaste for discussing the human limitations of him who is our Lord. It is hard to participate in such a discussion without seeming insufferably arrogant and without offending against the respect, nay adoration, that the figure of Jesus Christ calls forth. Nevertheless, the discussion is going on, and for the exegete not to participate would be a neglect of duty.

Dogmatic theologians, not exegetes, have led the way in the modern discussion of Jesus' human knowledge.[2] If exegetes had begun the discussion, the orientation might have been different. They would probably have tended to

[1] This chapter was given in preliminary form at Denver in June, 1965, at the Twentieth Annual Convention of the Catholic Theological Society. Despite the kind encouragement of Father Gerald Van Ackeren, the president of the Society, I was unable to put the paper into final form in time to have it included in the *Proceedings*. I still wish to thank the Theological Society for their sensitivity in inviting one involved in biblical studies to treat such an important theological question.

[2] The theologians found most helpful include: A. Durand, "La science du Christ," *Nouvelle Revue Théologique* 71 (1949) 497–503; K. Rahner, "Dogmatic Considerations on Knowledge and Consciousness in Christ," *Dogmatic vs. Biblical Theology*, ed. by H. Vorgrimler (Baltimore: Helicon, 1964), pp. 241–267; J. Galot, "Science et conscience de Jésus," *Nouvelle Revue Théologique* 82 (1960) 113–131; B. Lonergan, *De Verbo Incarnato* (3rd ed.; Rome: Gregorian, 1964) pp. 332–416. Interesting surveys are T. E. Clarke, "Some Aspects of Current Christology," *Thought* 36 (1961) 325–343; E. Gutwenger, "The Problem of Christ's Knowledge," *Concilium* 11 (1966: *Who is Jesus of Nazareth?*) 91–105.

39

start with Heb 4:15 which describes Jesus as "one who has been tempted as we are in every respect, yet without sinning." As Chalcedon (DBS 301) rightly recognized, this means that Jesus is "consubstantial with us according to humanity, similar to us in all things except sin." Ignorance does not seem to be excluded by such a statement; and while there are other statements in the New Testament that do seem to reject any ignorance on Jesus' part, an exegete working from the evidence supplied by his own field would not have any a priori inclination against seeing limitation in Jesus' knowledge. But the modern discussion that theologians have taken up was already oriented by the medieval theory that Jesus possessed different types of extraordinary knowledge that prevented limitation.[3] The guiding principle that had come down to the theologians was not Heb 4:15 but: "One cannot deny to Christ any perfection that it was possible for him to have had." One can only admire the openness of modern theologians who had the intellectual courage to re-examine these earlier positions that seemed to foreclose any discussion of limitation. Moreover, they have had to re-evaluate the many statements of the Church on this question, most of them quite unfavorable to limitation;[4] and only after a very care-

[3] Besides experimental knowledge it has been customary to attribute to Jesus: (a) Beatific knowledge. Jesus would know in the divine essence all that God would know by the scientia visionis. The primary object known in beatific vision is God Himself; the secondary object consists of created realities seen in God. (b) Infused knowledge. Jesus had a passive intellect which was activated in plenitude by infusion. This would be a knowledge comparable to angelic knowledge.

[4] In 1918 the Holy Office (DBS 3645) said that one could not safely teach that during his life Christ did not have in his soul the same knowledge that the blessed possess. In Mystici Corporis Pius XII (DBS 3812) said that Christ enjoyed the beatific vision from virtually [vixdum] the first moment he was in Mary's womb. In 1907 Pius X (DBS 3434) condemned the Modernist proposition that the critical scholar cannot ascribe to Christ unlimited knowledge; see also n. 64 below. For early papal statements about Jesus' knowledge of the Parousia see n. 59

ful historical investigation about what was condemned in the past (and under what circumstances and modality) have they evolved their own theories of Christ's knowledge, theories which, they claim, legitimately allow limitation.

Much that is pertinent biblically to the question of Jesus' knowledge, especially of his knowledge of himself, has been written by Protestant exegetes. However, since they approach the problem without the particular theological background that looms so large in the Catholic study of the problem, their work has been of only limited help to Catholic theologians. Exegetical studies by Catholics of the problem of Jesus' knowledge have been relatively few;[5] yet it is just such study that would be of most help to the theologians. One reason for the paucity of these studies is that truly critical New Testament exegesis has, with some important exceptions, been a reality in Catholic circles only in the past few years; and only critical exegesis would see the limitations attributed to Jesus in the earliest layers of New Testament tradition. Another reason, however, has been the repercussions that such studies might bring upon their writers, for they leave the writers open to the charge of denying the divinity of Jesus.[6] This is somewhat para-

---

below. Pope Gregory the Great (DBS 476) would seem to have ruled out even acquired human knowledge; for he assures us that when Jesus asked where the women had laid the body of Lazarus (Jn 11:34), it was not because he did not know where the grave was!

[5] Bibliography is given in R. Schnackenburg, New Testament Theology Today (New York: Herder and Herder, 1963), p. 60; but he admits that almost all the work is apologetic in character and not really biblical. The most important critical contribution is A. Vögtle, "Exegetische Erwägungen über das Wissen und Selbstbewusstsein Jesu," Gott in Welt (K. Rahner Festschrift; Freiburg: Herder, 1964) pp. 608–667. There are also some Catholic studies of individual titles given to Jesus. In English-speaking Catholic literature we are singularly poor on this subject.

[6] In the July 24, 1966 questionnaire sent by the Doctrinal Congregation (Holy Office) to the Bishops (AAS 58 [1966] 660), point 5 of the possible dangers stated: "There is afoot a certain christological humanism that would reduce Christ to the condition of a mere man, who gradually

doxical, because only when one has a strong faith in the divinity of Jesus is there a real problem about admitting that his knowledge might have been limited. Those who think of him as a mere man have no problem: his knowledge could not be anything but limited.

But Catholic exegetes must put aside fear of misunderstanding and misrepresentation and take up the study. This is urgent *first* because they have a duty toward theology. As we shall insist in the conclusion, the biblical evidence does not decide the theological problem or conclusively support one theory over another. Yet the theologians who are trying bravely to establish the possibility of new answers must have available to them competent critical surveys of the New Testament evidence in order to see how their theories can be best reconciled with this evidence. Exegetical study is urgent *second* because, in the absence of careful treatments, facile and inexact estimates of the New Testament picture are circulating among the Catholic public.[7] *Newsweek* of April 11, 1966 attributed to Catholic scholars two statements on this question — statements of a type heard

became conscious of his divine Sonship." It is not clear whether the Holy Office was maintaining that all theories of gradual development of consciousness would reduce Christ to a mere man, or was objecting only to such theories of gradual development of consciousness as would reduce Christ to a mere man. It will become apparent in the chapter that I think there is no real biblical evidence for such gradual development of *consciousness*; yet Catholics who hold such a theory do not by any means reduce Christ to a mere man. The reply to this questionnaire by the French Bishops (Dec. 17, 1966) answered this point admirably: "The recent labors of exegesis make it necessary for us to deepen the knowledge of the man Christ without compromising faith in his divinity" (*Catholic Messenger* of Davenport, March 2, 1967, p. 5).

[7] To a certain extent this is the result of instructing Catholic biblical scholars not to discuss delicate subjects on a popular level. All that this accomplishes is to leave popularization in the hands of those who are not scholars. We simply have to face the fact that the discussion of delicate subjects cannot be kept from the public. What is discussed in a highly professional meeting today will appear in *Time* or the *National Catholic Reporter* tomorrow. This may not be for the best interests of theological science, but it is the factual situation.

by the present writer from many questioners in many parts
of the country. One was: "Jesus had to discover who he
was. He was uncertain of his divine sonship; yet he never
abandoned his quest for certainty"; the other was: "I'm
sure that Jesus himself was not aware of being God."[8]
As will become apparent in the course of this essay, I
do not believe that scientific biblical study can substan-
tiate either of these statements; but we must write to that
effect or such evaluations will carry the day. Exegetical
study of Jesus' knowledge is demanded for a *third* and
final reason: many problems in the history of New Testament thought can be solved only if we know to what
extent Jesus' own knowledge of these problems was limited.
How can we trace through the New Testament a gradual
development in the understanding of such topics as Jesus'
divinity, the personality of the Spirit, the organization of
the Church, eschatology, etc., unless we know whether or
not Jesus' formulations about them might have been un-
clear and limited? In other words, the failure to tackle the
problem of Jesus' knowledge is holding up progress in
other New Testament fields.

The present chapter will to the extent of my ability be
an exercise of *critical* exegesis and will admit the possibility
that statements attributed to Jesus by the evangelists were
not uttered by him or have been substantially modified.
Despite the fact that Vatican II gave approval to such exegesis in principle,[9] many still feel uneasy when a statement
is treated in this way; and so at times I shall lean over
backward to see what would be the implication if a dubious

[8] The first statement was attributed to Father John Dunne (see n. 39
below); the second (see n. 88) to Brother Isadore McCarran. Of course,
no one would hold either man responsible for statements reported out of
context in a "news" magazine.

[9] In the Constitution *De Revelatione*, 4, 19, while the historical
character of the Gospels is asserted, it is recognized that what Jesus

statement really were the words of Jesus. In cases where no firm decision about *ipsissima verba* can be reached, I shall often comment on what the statements attributed to Jesus tell us about the evangelists' attitude toward his knowledge. Although all the texts dealing with the subject cannot be treated in short short a space, I have made a real effort to cover the most important and representative ones. In view of the delicacy of the subject matter, I wish to state that I am completely open to correction if my evaluation of the evidence is unsatisfactory either exegetically or because of theological implications. There has been an attempt to combine honesty with circumspection, precisely because I am mindful of the caution the Church has shown in questions of Christ's knowledge. The non-Catholic reader will have to make the effort to understand the treatment in the light of the Catholic problematic.

This study will necessarily seem pointless or objectionable only to the theological positions at the two ends of the spectrum. To the absolute minimalist who thinks that Jesus knew no more than any other man, the attempt to leave place for the divine in his consciousness will seem forced. To the absolute maximalist who says that Jesus was God and therefore knew everything that God knows, the uncovering of evidence of limitation will seem blasphemous.[10] To all the more nuanced positions in between[11] the study

said and did underwent several stages of modification. It was preached by the apostles; then it was selected, synthesized, and explained by the evangelists. Obviously, such a process means that we do not always have the *ipsissima verba* of Jesus.

[10] Often such a position represents inaccurate theology. The divine nature and the human nature in Christ remain distinct. St. Thomas (*Summa Theologica* III, q. 9, a. 1, ad 1) says: "If there had not been in the soul of Christ some other knowledge besides his divine knowledge, he would not have known anything. Divine knowledge cannot be an act of the human soul of Christ; it belongs to another nature."

[11] Almost all Catholic scholars today admit a limited experiential knowledge on Jesus' part. Few would follow the Salmanticenses (*Cursus*

will offer evidence that must be faced. If the study has the byproduct of making Jesus seem more human, this too can be a service to Christian truth. It was Pope Leo the Great[12] who said, "It is as dangerous an evil to deny the truth of the human nature in Christ as to refuse to believe that his glory is equal to that of his Father."

I. JESUS' KNOWLEDGE OF THE ORDINARY AFFAIRS OF LIFE

There are texts in the Gospels that seem to indicate that Jesus shared normal human ignorance about the affairs of life; there are other texts that attribute to him extraordinary and even superhuman knowledge about such affairs.

A. Texts indicating ignorance

1. The best example from the public ministry is Mk 5:30–33. Jesus has been walking through a crowd; a woman touches his garments and is healed by his miraculous power. Perceiving that power has gone forth from him, Jesus asks who touched his garments. The disciples think that this is a foolish question when there has been so much pushing and pulling in the crowd; but the woman comes forward and confesses. The narrative seems clearly to presuppose ignorance on Jesus' part.[13]

Theologicus, tractatus XXI "De Incarnatione," disp. 22, dubium 2, n. 29) who maintained that among men Jesus was the greatest dialectician, philosopher, mathematician, doctor, politician, musician, orator, painter, farmer, sailor, soldier, etc.

[12] *Sermon 7 on the Nativity* (PL 54,216): "Paris enim periculi malum est: si illi autem naturae nostrae veritas aut paternae gloriae negatur aequalitas."

[13] The story is roughly the same in Lk 8:45–47, but Mt 9:22 leaves out the description of Jesus' question and his search. In Mt, Jesus turns,

2. There are two texts in Luke's infancy narrative that deserve attention. In Lk 2:46 Jesus is shown in the Temple at the age of twelve asking questions of the teachers of the Law. The next verse says that the teachers were amazed at his understanding and at the answers he gave. Jesus is evidently thought of as a precocious boy, anxious to learn. In Lk 2:52, after the above scene, Jesus is described as growing in wisdom, as well as in stature and the favor of God. This is a stereotyped formula, for a similar statement is made about Samuel in 1 Sm 2:26 and of John the Baptist in Lk 1:80. From a critical viewpoint these texts are difficult to use in a reconstruction of Jesus' life, for there is no *scientific* way of verifying the material in Luke's infancy narrative (there is no comparative material; we know nothing of Luke's source). Yet it is clear that the evangelist did not think it strange that Jesus should ask questions or grow in knowledge. This is an important consideration precisely because Luke's infancy narrative presents Jesus as God's Son from the first moment of his conception.

B. *Texts indicating extraordinary or superhuman knowledge*

1. There is a tendency in the later Gospels to suppress any suggestion that Jesus had to gain ordinary knowledge. We have already seen this in Mt (note 13), but it is especially true of Jn. If in Jn 6:5 Jesus asks Philip where bread can be found to feed the large crowd, the parenthet-

---

sees the woman, and knows what has happened. Obviously, the Marcan form is more original, and Mt reflects an uneasiness about the ignorance that Mk attributes to Jesus. A similar corrective attitude toward other "human weaknesses" reported in the Marcan account is seen, for instance, in Mt's omission of the miracle where Jesus' attempt to heal a blind man is at first only partially successful (Mk 8:22–26), and in Mt's toning down of the gruff attitude of the disciples toward Jesus (cf. Mt 8:25 with Mk 4:38).

ical addition in the next verse insists that Jesus was only testing Philip, for Jesus already knew what he was going to do. If Jesus chooses some disciples of poor quality, nevertheless, he knew from the beginning those who would refuse to believe (6:64). In particular, he knew that Judas Iscariot would betray him (6:71;13:11). All of this is part of the Johannine tendency to picture Jesus without any element of human weakness or dependence (10:18; cf 4:2 with 3:23). Although John insists that the word became flesh (1:14), E. Käsemann is right when he says that the Johannine Jesus has not undergone a kenosis, i.e., taken the form of a servant. In the incarnate Jesus the glory of God's own Son constantly shines forth for all who have eyes to see.[14]

2. All the Gospels attribute to Jesus the ability to know what men are thinking even though they have not expressed themselves (Mk 2:6–8 and par.; Mk 9:33–34 with Lk 9:46–47; Jn 2:24–25; 16:19 and 30). One might question whether this ability, if historical, represented a keen perception of human nature or a superhuman knowledge. Certainly in Jn, and perhaps in the other Gospels as well, the evangelist seems to suppose the latter.

3. All the Gospels have incidents wherein Jesus knows what is happening elsewhere, beyond the limits of human sight.
— In Jn 1:48–49 Jesus knows what Nathanael has been doing under the fig tree, much to Nathanael's amazement.
— In Mk 11:2 and par., as Jesus prepares to enter Jerusalem, he instructs the disciples to go into a nearby village;

[14] In *Interpretation* 21 (Oct. 1967) we discuss Käsemann's latest book, *Jesu letzter Wille nach Johannes 17* (Tübingen: Mohr, 1966). There are exaggerations in it, but in honesty one must admit that taken alone the Johannine portrait of Jesus is somewhat onesided in favor of divinity. Only by balancing Jn with Mk do we have the scriptural basis for considering Jesus both fully divine and fully human.

at the entrance they will find a colt tied on which no one has ever sat (Mt has two animals).[15] This story is not recounted in Jn, whose narrative of the entry into Jerusalem is in some respects more primitive than that of the Synoptics. In Jn 12:14 Jesus himself finds the animal.

— In Mk 14:13-14 and Lk 22:10 as preparation for Passover Jesus sends two of his disciples with the instruction: "Go into the city and a man carrying a water jar will meet you; follow him and wherever he enters say to the householder, 'The Teacher says, "Where is my guest room where I am to eat the Passover with my disciples?" ' " It will be noted that the account in Mt 26:18 has no such hint of mysterious knowledge of what is about to happen. The Matthean Jesus simply directs the disciples to go to a certain man's house to make the Passover arrangements.

— In Mt 17:24-27 Jesus tells Peter to go to the Lake of Galilee and the first fish that he catches will have a shekel in its mouth. We are never told that Peter did as instructed, but that is the implication of the story. This story is found only in Mt, probably stemming from the peculiarly Matthean Petrine source (14:28-33; 16:16b-19). Its main purpose is didactic (problem of paying taxes; association of Peter and Jesus); Jesus' knowledge that the coin would be in the fish's mouth is incidental. It is a most difficult miracle story, for it is one of the few miracles of Jesus that closely resemble magical action, worthy of the popular tales of the Hellenistic miracle-workers. Many scholars would regard it as a popular tale.

In discussing this third group of incidents, we find it

---

[15] One might argue in this instance and in the one we shall mention next that Jesus had previously arranged with the necessary people what would happen, but the evangelists scarcely interpreted the event in such a rationalistic way. They saw these as instances of extraordinary knowledge.

difficult to obtain scientific assurance of the historical value of the versions in which Jesus exhibits superhuman knowledge. The first and fourth incidents have no other verification, and the fourth is extremely difficult. In the second and third incidents there is another version that supposes no extraordinary knowledge. Despite this difficulty, were we to decide that the tradition of Jesus' ability to know what is happening elsewhere does go back to early tradition, we should still be careful about any theological assumption that would trace such knowledge to the hypostatic union or to the beatific vision. The Old Testament attributes this type of knowledge to many prophets, e.g., Ezekiel living in Babylon has visions of events occurring in Jerusalem. Extrasensory sight at a distance is supposed in a story about Samuel (1 Sm 10:1 ff.) that is very similar to the incident of Mk 14 cited above.

To sum up, there is an ancient Gospel tradition that accepts without noticeable difficulty normal ignorance on Jesus' part of the ordinary affairs of life; the suppression of this by Mt and Jn is a secondary theological modification. On the other hand, probably as far back as one can trace the tradition, Jesus was presented as a man with more than ordinary knowledge and perception about other men. The latter feature does not exclude the former in great religious and prophetical figures, and thus a combination of the two is almost to be expected in Jesus.

II. JESUS' GENERAL KNOWLEDGE
OF RELIGIOUS MATTERS

What we have said in the previous section would not offer difficulty to most dogmatic theologians, for there are few today who do not admit that Jesus had to gain experimental knowledge in ordinary affairs. Many, however, would not admit ignorance of religious matters.[16] We are touching here on the substance of Jesus' ministry or, at least, of the Gospel accounts of that ministry, for these documents report only what is of religious import — humdrum things done by Jesus that had little or no religious significance are passed over.[17] (If in the previous section we saw examples of extraordinary knowledge in ordinary affairs, even those incidents were ultimately associated with an action that had religious significance.) Leaving aside for the moment all questions about Jesus' knowledge of himself and of his mission in relation to the kingdom of God, we shall concentrate here on his general religious knowledge. In the use of the Scriptures and of theological concepts did Jesus manifest a knowledge far beyond that of his time, so that one would be forced to posit a supernatural source for this knowledge?

A. Jesus' knowledge of the Scriptures

The Scriptures supplied the basic religious vocabulary of Judaism; and if Jesus had extraordinary knowledge, we would expect it to be manifest here. While we shall cite below the instances in the Gospels where Jesus is said to have used Scripture, we must caution that it is very difficult to be certain we are dealing with *ipsissima verba*. One of the prominent features in the apostolic preaching was the introduction of an Old Testament background that would make Jesus intelligible to his fellow Jews. Such a resort to

[16] Yet K. Rahner, art. cit., p. 261, says: "We may speak without any embarrassment of a spiritual, indeed religious development of Jesus."

[17] The same thing happened, of course, with the great figures of the Old Testament and with Paul, and so we constantly have an idealized picture of men whose every thought and action centered around God and His work in the world.

the Old Testament was almost certainly in continuity with Jesus' own custom of citing the Scriptures, but it is not always possible to determine whether the Gospel reference to the Old Testament stems from Jesus or from the apostolic preaching.

1. There are instances where the citation of Scripture attributed to Jesus involves a mistake. We shall not bother with incidents where he cites Scripture and no such citation can be found in the Old Testament, e.g., Jn 7:38. In such instances there is always the possibility that he is citing a book that has not been preserved for us,[18] or that he is citing a targum or some other popular form of the biblical text.

— In Mk 2:26 Jesus says that David entered the house of God when Abiathar was high priest and ate the loaves of the presence. The scene is found in 1 Sm 21:1-6, but there the high priest is not Abiathar but Ahimelech.[19] Abiathar was better known than Ahimelech and more closely associated with David in later life, so that popular tradition may have easily confused the two. But if the reading is genuine, Jesus shows no awareness that he is following an inaccurate version of the story.

— In Mt 23:35 Jesus refers to all the guiltless blood shed on earth from the blood of Abel to the blood of Zechariah the son of Barachiah who was murdered between the sanctuary and the altar. This identification of Zechariah seems

[18] The canon of sacred Jewish books had not yet been established, at least in the area of "The Writings." The Jews of Jesus' time, e.g. at Qumrân and at Alexandria, used books as sacred that subsequent Jewish tradition did not canonize.

[19] Mt and Lk seem to have noticed the difficulty, for their accounts of this saying of Jesus omit any mention of the high priest (Mt 12:4; Lk 6:4). Some mss. of Mk also omit the italicized phrase, but the better mss. and the rules of textual criticism favor genuineness.

to represent a confusion.[20] Zechariah the son of Barachiah was a minor prophet who flourished ca. 520–516, but it was Zechariah the son of Jehoiada who was killed in the Temple ca. 825 B.C. (2 Chr 24:20–22).

2. There are instances where the citation of Scripture attributed to Jesus shows no critical sense but reflects the mistaken ideas of his time.

— In Mk 12:36 and par. Jesus cites Ps 110 ("The Lord said to my Lord") and attributes this psalm to David. This is not just a general attribution, for Jesus' whole argument rests on the fact that David himself composed the psalm.[21] Most modern scholars, Catholics included, think of the psalm as one uttered by a proclaimer of royal oracles at the coronation or anniversary of the king. Personal authorship by David is most unlikely.

— In Mt 12:39–41 (also 16:4; Lk 11:29–32) Jesus says that the sign of Jonah the prophet will be given to the present generation. If we leave aside the question of what the sign was, his reference to the Book of Jonah is best understood if he thought of it as a historical account. Indeed, conservative scholars have used Jesus' citation to prove that Jonah is historical, despite the improbable events narrated therein. Modern scholars, however, are almost unanimous in identifying Jonah as a parable built up around the figure of the unknown prophet, Jonah the son of Amittai (2 Kg 14:25). Nevertheless, we should not

[20] Apparently Lk was aware of this, for Lk 11:51 does not have the words "the son of Barachiah." Lest we dismiss such confusion of characters as insignificant, let us remember that one of the standard Christian arguments against the sacred, revealed character of the Koran has been that Mohammed seems to have confused Miriam the sister of Moses with Miriam (Mary) the mother of Jesus.

[21] Of course, for a long time Jesus' attribution of the psalm to David was taken as incontrovertible proof that David did write the psalm, e.g., the decree of the Biblical Commission of May 1, 1910 (*EB²* #348). For Catholic freedom in such matters now see *Catholic Biblical Quarterly* 18 (1956) 24–25.

put too much emphasis on this example because we cannot be *certain* that Jesus treated Jonah as historical.

3. In still other instances the citations of Scripture attributed to Jesus employ a hermeneutic that would be judged unacceptable today, for it violates the literal sense of the passage. Interpretation that goes beyond the literal was quite customary in Jesus' time, e.g., in the Qumrân writings, in the targums, and in the rabbinical writings; but here we are asking precisely whether Jesus demonstrated a knowledge of Scripture beyond that of his day.

— In Jn 10:33–36, in order to refute the Jews who accuse him of making himself God, Jesus cites Ps 82:6 which speaks of the judges as "gods." Thus he argues that the Jewish Scriptures themselves use the title "god" for men. There are many attempts to explain such exegesis,[22] but it seems inescapable that Jesus is glossing over a difference in meaning in the word "god." The Jews have accused him of making himself God with a capital "g"; he has answered by pointing to an example where men are called "gods" in an applied sense. Yet, since this scene is so redolent of Johannine theology, we cannot use it with any scientific assurance that the citation represents *ipsissima verba*.

— If we return to Mk 12:36 and par., we find another hermeneutic problem in Jesus' insistence that Ps 110 refers to the Messiah. He presumes that in "The Lord [= God] said to my Lord" the "my Lord" is the Messiah. Few modern scholars, Catholics included, would think that there was an expectation of "the Messiah" when Ps 110 was composed.[23] The Pharisees were not able to refute Jesus' argu-

---

[22] For the most important theories see *The Gospel According to John I-XII* (Anchor Bible; New York: Doubleday, 1966) pp. 409–411.

[23] See J. A. Fitzmyer, "The Son of David Tradition and Matthew 22, 41–46 and Parallels," *Concilium* 20 (1967: *The Dynamism of Biblical Tradition*) 75–87.

ment since, seemingly, they too thought that the psalm referred to the Messiah; but if taken *literally*, Ps 110 would not establish Jesus' point.

In summing up, we should also recall that there are Gospel passages which portray Jesus as learned in Scripture. A general admiration of the authority and depth of Jesus' teaching is reported (Mt 7:29; 22:16), and in particular Jn 7:15 seems to relate this astonishment to his knowledge of Scripture.[24] The Gospels present Jesus as not hesitating to contradict current exegesis when such exegesis conflicted with his own interpretation of his role or of the demands of the kingdom of God.[25] Yet in questions of authorship, literary form, historicity, and principles of hermeneutics, the Jesus of the Gospels reflects the often inadequate and even erroneous ideas of his time.

B. *Jesus' use of contemporary religious concepts*

Here obviously we must be selective. If we are inquiring about the knowledge of Jesus, the most useful field of study would be his attitude toward the concepts of his time that by common consent we now consider inadequate or incorrect. Did he demonstrate an awareness of this inadequacy, as we might expect if he were omniscient? Certainly he is presented in the Gospels as correcting or modifying ideas of his time that were intimately involved

[24] "How did this fellow get his education when he had no teacher?" — a knowledge of how to read and write was centered about a knowledge of the Scriptures, for that is what children were trained to read. Lk 4:17 also has the tradition that Jesus could read the Bible.

[25] His citation of Ps 110, for instance, is to prove that the exegesis of the Pharisees is wrong: the Messiah is more than the Son of David. See also the series: "You have heard it said . . . but I say to you" (Mt 5).

with his own mission (ideas about the Messiah, the Son
of Man, etc.) or with God's demand on man (ideas of
morality, marriage, ritual purity, brotherly love, etc.). But
for the moment we are concerned with Jesus' attitude
toward general religious concepts that were not so intimately involved in his mission. We shall discuss demonology, the picture of the afterlife, and apocalyptic.

1. *Demonology*. The Gospels describe an extraordinary
number of cases of demon possession during the ministry
of Jesus. We are not proposing here to question the existence of the demons, or the possibility of demon possession, or even that demon possession may have been more
frequent before the kingdom of God made its inroads on
the kingdom of evil. But some of the cases that the
Synoptic Gospels describe as instances of demon possession
seem to be instances of natural sickness. The symptoms
described in Mk 9:17-18 seem to be those of epilepsy,
while the symptoms in Mk 5:4 seem to be those of dangerous insanity. One cannot escape the impression that
sometimes in speaking of demon possession the evangelists are reflecting the inexact medico-religious understanding of their times. But in the scenes mentioned Jesus
himself is portrayed as dealing with demon possession. In
the second instance he drives the demons out of the insane
man into a herd of swine — another instance of popular
ideas of demonology. The parable attributed to Jesus in
the "Q" tradition (Mt 12:43-45; Lk 11:24-26) about the
demons wandering around looking for a place to dwell is
still another example of primitive ideas. Jesus occasionally
corrects the ideas of his time about too close a relationship
between sickness or calamity and personal sin (Lk 13:1-4;
Jn 9:2-3), but in the general Gospel picture there is no
indication that in the questions of demons and of the

sickness caused by them he saw the inadequacies of the popular views of his time.[26]

2. *Afterlife.* Jesus is not reported to have given detailed descriptions of the afterlife. Was this because it was not his mission to reveal such things, or because he did not know details about the afterlife? Scientifically we cannot answer that question, but we can evaluate the materialistic images that he uses in the few instances where he does speak of the subject. In Mk 9:43 ff. Jesus describes men as entering the next life with one hand, one foot, or one eye, as if in the future life men were to possess bodies such as they have on earth, even with defects. Punishment is described in terms of unquenchable fire (Mk 9:48; Mt 25:41), ravenous worms (Mk 9:48), frustrated grinding of teeth and weeping (Mt 8:12; 13:42), and insatiable thirst (Lk 16:24). A great chasm separates the place of beatitude from the place of fiery punishment (Lk 16:26). In the place of beatitude men enjoy sumptuous banquets in the presence of God and the patriarchs (Mt 8:11), while the envious damned are compelled to witness (Lk 13:28). Besides the difficulty of determining whether such descriptions represent *ipsissima verba* or not, we face here the added problem of determining how much of this language Jesus meant as figurative. On the one hand, we cannot assume that all of it was meant literally, and on the other we cannot assume that Jesus shared our own sophistication on some of these questions. If Jesus speaks of heaven above the clouds (Mk 13:26; 14:62), how can we be sure that he knew that it was not above the clouds? The fact that in one instance he corrected a popular view of the afterlife with which he did not agree (Mk 12:25

[26] It is true that the Fourth Gospel describes no instances of demon possession, but this is scarcely a primitive trait preserved only in Jn..

and par.: the resurrected dead will not marry) might suggest that he had no objection to the other popular views that colored his own language.

A related question would concern Jesus' knowledge of the immortality of the soul.[27] Certainly most of Jesus' references to the afterlife were in terms of the resurrection of the body. Yet the picture is not so simple as sometimes expressed by popularizers of modern Catholic biblical thought. Passages like Mk 8:36, Mt 10:28, and Lk 23:43 are more easily explained if ideas of an immortal soul were already known in Palestine. J. Barr[28] may be correct in insisting that both resurrection of the body and immortality of the soul were Gospel anticipations. Therefore, we should be careful in assuming that Jesus showed no knowledge of something so fundamental to the afterlife as immortality.[29]

[27] O. Cullmann, *Immortality of the Soul or Resurrection of the Dead* (London: Epworth, 1958) has argued strongly that the New Testament hope is not one of immortality; a fortiori he would argue that Jesus did not preach immortality.

[28] *Old and New in Interpretation* (London: SCM, 1966), pp. 52 ff.

[29] Leaving aside the question of whether Cullmann or Barr is right about the New Testament hope, we would still reject the thesis of Cullmann that subsequent Christians should not insist on immortality of the soul because the New Testament did not propose this doctrine. His thesis is in agreement with his principle that all truly normative revelation is to be found in the Scriptures, a principle that, personally, I cannot accept even in the mitigated form which some Roman Catholics are now propounding. If Vatican II was wise in rejecting a two-source formula (all revelation may be found in Scripture and in Tradition, conceived as separate sources), it was just as wise in not phrasing its statement on the subject in terms of an exclusively "in Scripture" formula. Revelation involves God's *action* for the salvation of men and the *interpretation* of that action by men whom God has raised up and guided for that purpose — in short, it involves both deeds and words motivated by God. Now the truly revelatory action of God bringing about the salvation of men is found in what He has done in Israel and what He has done in Jesus, and this action is described in the books of Scripture. Scripture also offers an *interpretation* of that action (e.g., the interpretation of the Sinai covenant by the prophets, and the interpretation of Jesus' mission by himself and by the apostles). This scriptural interpretation of God's revelatory action is the most important and essential interpretation; it is

3. *Apocalyptic.* The problem that we faced in eval-
uating the figurative language attributed to Jesus in
describing the afterlife is the same that we face in eval-
uating the apocalyptic language found in Jesus' descriptions
of the end of time. We hear that the sun and moon will
be darkened and the stars will fall down from heaven
(Mk 13:24-25 and par.); there will be earthquakes, fam-
ine, and wars (Mk 13:7-8 and par.) — in short, all the
phenomena that Jewish apocalyptic had been predicting
for centuries. Of course, we do not know that such things
will not happen, but few scholars would be willing to
accept such imagery as more than a stereotyped description
of catastrophe, a description that had become so much a
part of apocalyptic that one could not otherwise describe
the final divine intervention. If these apocalyptic descriptions in the Gospel go back to Jesus himself,[30] he would

---

an interpretation that should guide all subsequent interpretation, so that
there is an enduring responsibility to Scripture. But the scriptural interpretation is still a limited interpretation; it reflects the understanding of
God's action in a period that extends approximately from 1000 B.C. to
A.D. 125. God's action for the salvation of men came to a climax in
Jesus Christ who is once and for all (*eph hapax:* Heb 10:10), but there
is no reason to believe that God has ceased to guide the interpretation
of that action. Indeed, the subsequent role of the Spirit in the history
of the Church and in the history of men, the writings of the Fathers
and theologians, the pronouncements of the Church — all of these enter
into what we call Tradition, which is the post-scriptural interpretation of
the salvific action of God described in Scripture. If one has to propose
a formula describing where one can find revelation, instead of saying that
all revelation is in Scripture, I would prefer to say: "The revelation of
God to men is found in God's action on behalf of man's salvation,
as that action is interpreted by the Scriptures themselves and by later
authoritative Tradition." The importance of Scripture is that it contains
both the narrative of that action and the fundamental interpretation of
that action, but there can be subsequent *normative* interpretation of
God's action that is not found in Scripture. The doctrine of the Assumption is a normative interpretation of what God has done in Jesus Christ,
but that interpretation is not found in Scripture.

[30] A principle often espoused by German critics is that any Gospel
material with close parallels in contemporary Jewish thought is not scientifically verifiable as coming authentically from Jesus. Such material could
have been added by the early Christian preachers under Jewish influence.

certainly have been conscious that he was repeating stylized language. Yet once again, there is nothing in these passages to suggest that Jesus did not expect the phenomena he described.

To sum up, in the three areas of demonology, the afterlife, and apocalyptic, Jesus seems to draw on the imperfect religious concepts of his time without indication of superior knowledge and without substantially correcting the concepts. Once more, to prevent confusion, we emphasize that there is an important religious area where the teaching attributed to Jesus was unique, outdistancing the ideas of his time — the area of his own mission and the proclamation of the kingdom of God. But we do not find a uniqueness in the broad religious concepts we have been discussing in this section.

III. JESUS' KNOWLEDGE OF THE FUTURE

In this field of inquiry we come closer to the area that we have just described as unique. To a certain extent a knowledge of the future might be expected of Jesus since he was described as a prophet (Mk 6:15; Lk 7:16; Jn 6:14).[31] It is is a commonplace of modern biblical science that the prophets of the Old Testament were primarily religious reformers involved with their own times who did not spend their lives gazing into the distant future in the manner once thought. Therefore, in such an understanding of a prophet, Jesus the prophet would not necessarily have

Under such a stringent criterion apocalyptic material would certainly be suspect. Most Catholics, however, prefer the principle that the Gospel material is innocent until proven guilty, rather than vice versa. It should be accepted as authentic unless there is a reason to the contrary.

[31] It is quite plausible that Jesus was thought of as a prophet during his ministry, for the role of prophet was a much more spontaneously obvious one than the roles implied in some of the other titles that the Gospels give Jesus (Messiah, Son of Man, etc.).

had foreknowledge. But we cannot judge the first-century estimation of Jesus as a prophet from the standpoint of a modern critical understanding of the Old Testament prophet. In post-biblical Judaism a notion of prophecy had evolved that stressed the prophetic foreknowledge of the future. The Qumrân *pesharim* or biblical interpretations suppose that prophets like Habakkuk were really writing about the Qumrân community which did not appear till hundreds of years after the prophets' time. Therefore, Jesus' contemporaries' evaluation of him as a prophet may well have connoted a tradition that he knew the future.[32]

But there are difficulties in determining from the Gospels whether and to what extent Jesus actually did know the future. The Gospels were written *after* most of the events that Jesus is thought to have predicted — all were written after his death and resurrection; Mt, Lk, and Jn were probably written after the fall of Jerusalem. In order to indicate the fulfillment of Jesus' words, the Gospel writers may have clarified those words so that the reader would recognize their nature as prophecy.[33] Consequently, in the prophecies attributed to Jesus, how much represents the *ipsissima verba* and how much represents clarification by the evangelist in the light of the subsequent event? If we do establish that the original statements of Jesus about the future may have been vaguer than they now appear, what is the demarcation line between firm conviction about how things will turn out and real foreknowledge? Genuine detailed foreknowledge is superhuman; unshakable conviction is not necessarily beyond human powers.

[32] Vatican I stated that Jesus did utter prophecies (*DBS* 3009).

[33] An older rationalist exegesis saw in these instances *vaticinia ex eventu* created by the Church or by the evangelists for apologetic purposes. We shall suggest that a truer emphasis might be achieved if we think of the evangelists or their predecessors clarifying what they saw as already a prophecy.

A. Foreknowledge of his own passion, crucifixion, and resurrection

All the Gospels attribute to Jesus such foreknowledge during his ministry. Yet there is a problem that might make us suspicious a priori of such exact predictions, namely, that the disciples who are supposed to have heard these predictions do not seem to have foreseen the crucifixion even when it was imminent nor to have expected the resurrection (Lk 24:19–26 is typical of the attitude found in all the Gospels). One may attribute this failure to the slowness of the disciples, but one may also wonder if the original predictions were as exact as they have now come to us.

— Mk 8:31; 9:31; 10:33–34 and par. On three occasions the Synoptic Gospels report sayings of Jesus foretelling his passion, death, and resurrection. In the first prediction Jesus says that the Son of Man (Mt: he) must suffer many things, be rejected by the elders and the chief priests and the scribes, be killed, and be raised after three days. The second prediction is less specific, for it simply speaks of action by men and does not mention the exact officials. The third prediction is the most specific; not only does it mention the officials, but it says that they will condemn him and deliver him to the Gentiles to be mocked, spit upon, and scourged. The Matthean form of the third prediction mentions crucifixion. These three sayings are Son of Man sayings of the variety that speak of the Son of Man as a suffering figure on earth. Neither of the two most recent full-scale treatises on the Son of Man[34] consider this class of Son of Man sayings to be genuine words

[34] H. E. Tödt, *The Son of Man in the Synoptic Tradition* (Philadelphia: Westminster, 1965); A. J. B. Higgins, *Jesus and the Son of Man* (Philadelphia: Fortress, 1964).

of Jesus. They point out that passages dealing with the suffering Son of Man are not found in the "Q" tradition and that for such sayings we have only the authority of the Marcan tradition. For Tödt, if Jesus spoke of a future coming of the Son of Man, he could not have described himself during his ministry as the Son of Man. But there are many other writers, including C. H. Dodd and C. F. D. Moule,[35] who think that suffering was associated with the Son of Man figure already in Dn 7. Thus the a priori case against the genuineness of the three sayings is far from certain.

The tradition of the three sayings is very ancient. Tödt himself has shown that the way they describe the passion, death, and resurrection does not come from the Marcan accounts of these events. In other words, the evangelist did not first compose an account of the passion, death, and resurrection and then go back and create the prophecies in light of his account; rather, the sayings came to Mk from a pre-Marcan Palestinian formulation. Have we then reason to suspect that these three sayings did not come from Jesus himself, once we have found inconclusive the argument against the genuineness of suffering Son of Man sayings? There is, of course, the general difficulty mentioned above about the failure of the disciples to understand after such explicit predictions. But there is also a problem created by the evidence of the Johannine tradition. John too has three predictions by Jesus that the Son of Man (or Jesus) must be crucified and raised up. In Jn 3:14 Jesus says: "The Son of Man must be lifted up" (also 8:28; 12:32). John makes clear that the phrase "lifted up" refers to the crucifixion, but there can be little doubt that the symbolism also includes

[35] See *Theology* 69 (1966) 174.

the resurrection-ascension.[36] But we note that the wording in the Johannine predictions has no details; rather, it echoes the vague language of Is 52:13: "Behold my servant . . . shall be lifted up." One might suggest that a similarly vague style of prediction lies behind the Synoptic sayings, perhaps also in Old Testament terms (if Dodd and Moule are right, then in terms of the suffering Son of Man from Dn 7). At least it would be easier to explain how the details were added *post eventum* in the Synoptic tradition than to postulate that they were lost in the Johannine tradition.

— In Jn 2:19 Jesus says to the Jewish authorities: "Destroy this Temple and in three days I will raise it up." The evangelist comments that he was talking about his body but that the disciples did not understand until after the resurrection. There is an echo of this saying in the Synoptic tradition (Mk 14:58; Mt 26:61; Mk 15:29; Mt 27:40), but there the verb is to *rebuild* rather than to *raise up*. Thus the interpretation of this saying as a prediction of Jesus' death and resurrection is peculiar to Jn and is dependent on the Johannine wording (which, at least in the use of "raise up," is certainly secondary).[37] The fact that a reference to three days appears in both the Synoptic and the Johannine form of the saying does not prove an allusion to Jesus' resurrection, for that phrase

[36] Anchor Bible, *John*, pp. 145–146.

[37] Far from being a clear prophecy, this saying seems to have been an embarrassment in the Synoptic tradition: Jesus had spoken about the destruction and rebuilding of the Temple, but he had died without the Temple's being destroyed or his rebuilding it. Lk omits the saying, but see Acts 6:14 where it is indirectly cited as still to be fulfilled. Mk 14:58 adds qualifications: "I will destroy this Temple *that is made with hands*, and in three days I will build another *not made with hands*." Mt 26:61 reduces the prediction to a possibility: "I *am able to* destroy the Temple of God and rebuild it in three days." Jn is giving us still another reinterpretation designed to remove the difficulty.

could mean simply a short time (Ex 19:11; Hos 6:2; Lk 13:32). Thus this logion cannot be used to establish Jesus' foreknowledge of his crucifixion and resurrection.

— In Mt 12:39–40 Jesus offers to the Pharisees the sign of Jonah: "As Jonah was three days and three nights in the belly of the whale, so will the Son of Man be three days and three nights in the heart of the earth." This is a clear prediction of the resurrection, but comparative Synoptic studies suggest that the Matthean interpretation of the sign is a secondary addition to a more original saying. In the parallel passage, Lk 11:29–30, 32, there is another interpretation of the sign, this time in terms of Jonah's preaching: "As Jonah became a sign to the men of Niniveh, so will the Son of Man be to this generation . . . for they repented at the preaching of Jonah" (the latter clause also appears in Mt 12:41, so Mt has elements of a twofold interpretation). A third form of the saying in Mt 16:4 simply mentions the sign without explaining it, and this may have been the original form of the logion. In that case the two different interpretations of the sign that now appear in Mt 12 and Lk 11 may represent alternative explanations current in the early Church — explanations that arose when Christians studied the career of Jonah to find out in what way Jonah was a sign of Jesus, the Son of Man. Thus, once again, this logion cannot be used to establish Jesus' foreknowledge of his resurrection.

— There is a tradition that Jesus knew beforehand that Judas would betray him. Jn 6:70–71 attributes this foreknowledge to Jesus during the ministry; all the Gospels (Mk 14:21 and par.; Jn 13:18, 21) report a prediction to this effect at the Last Supper, while Mk 14:41; Mt 26:45; and Jn 18:4 show Jesus aware of betrayal at Gethsemane. The last two groups of logia, at least in their Synoptic form, belong to the suffering Son of Man sayings (see the dispute mentioned above). If the agreement of the Synoptic and the Johannine tradition on the existence of such predictions offers at least a probability of their being original (perhaps without the title "Son of Man"), one may still wonder whether this prediction represents supernatural foreknowledge or only a penetrating insight into Judas' character and into the direction in which events were leading (especially if the prediction was made when the treason had already been committed). The evangelists seem to take the former option, but we may recall that Jn 12:6 describes Judas as previously corrupt.[38] In any case we could scarcely base a theory of Jesus' foreknowledge on these sayings alone.

Summing up the question of Jesus' foreknowledge of his passion, crucifixion, and resurrection, we find it difficult to be categorical. Modern criticism would cast doubt on a foreknowledge of the details, but we should not undervalue the general agreement of the Gospel tradition that Jesus was convinced beforehand that, while his life would be taken from him, God would ultimately vindicate him (see also Lk 17:25; Mk 10:45). It may be difficult to prove *scientifically* that any one saying represents the *ipsissima verba* of Jesus, but are we to suppose that this conviction about death and victory was spontaneously attributed to Jesus in the divergent traditions? One may argue that the attribution of predictive ability to Jesus was part of Church apologetics, but is it not just as reasonable to argue that the Church merely embellished with details a genuine tradition in which Jesus predicted that

[38] Yet the blackening of Judas' moral character in a late Gospel like Jn may well be a secondary trait.

he would die at the hands of men and be made victorious by God? Such a prediction could have come from his interpretation of the Old Testament (e.g., of Is, and perhaps of Dn) and would not presuppose superhuman knowledge. It could represent the unshakable conviction of a man who was sure that he knew God's plan. A similar conviction can be found in the career of Jeremiah and in Deutero-Isaiah's portrayal of the Servant.

If we suppose that beforehand Jesus had a conviction that God's victorious reign could be brought about only by his death, can anything be said about when he got such a conviction? Undoubtedly, Catholic writers of an earlier generation would have assumed that Jesus always knew he would have to die, but today some are beginning to suggest a psychological development of knowledge through various stages of the ministry. One popular thesis is that at first Jesus hoped to bring about God's reign through his preaching and miracles, but the discouragement of being rejected by the crowds and having the parables misunderstood led Jesus to realize that his own death would be required. J. S. Dunne[39] has suggested that it was probably when John the Baptist was killed by Herod that Jesus realized a similar fate awaited him.

While there is a certain attraction to such theses, since they fit Jesus into an understandable psychological pattern, we must recognize that there is simply no scientific way to prove them. They are really exercises of the imagination. For instance, the fact that in the Synoptic tradition (Mk 8:31 and par.) the first detailed prediction of death and resurrection occurs after the death of John the Baptist really proves nothing, for the form critical

[39] "The Human God: Jesus," *Commonweal* (February 10, 1967) 510. He promises a book developing the themes in this article.

analysis of the Gospels warns us against supposing that
the individual sayings of Jesus are reported in their original
sequence. And even if one argues that "substantially" the
Synoptic order is true to history, one must face the objection that there are in the Gospels vaguer but unmistakable
predictions of Jesus' death earlier in the ministry. We have
already seen that Jn records two predictions of death
(2:19–22; 3:14) before the arrest of the Baptist (see 3:24).
The Synoptics (Mk 2:20 and par.) also record a prediction before the death of the Baptist: "The day will come
when the bridegroom is taken away from them, and then
they will fast."[40] Cullmann[41] and many others think that
already from the time of his baptism the whole plan of
salvation was laid out before Jesus, including his death;
certainly the reference to "the lamb of God" in Jn 1:29
may be interpreted in this way.[42] Lk 2:33–35 would seem
to attribute a premonition of death to the period of Jesus'
infancy. We are not suggesting that these remembrances
of early predictions of death are necessarily historical —
some of them are not, and that is why, on the other side
of the question, the Gospels do not prove that Jesus always knew he would be put to death. But it is clear from
such passages that the evangelists were aware of no tradition that only late in his ministry did Jesus become aware

[40] V. Taylor, The Gospel According to St. Mark (London: Macmillan,
1953) 211–212 favors the authenticity of this saying, but thinks that the
incident originally may not have come so early in the ministry. In his
sequence the evangelist may be following a pre-Marcan tradition.

[41] The Christology of the New Testament (London: SCM, 1959) p.
67. One may doubt, however, whether in the Synoptic tradition of
the baptism there is really a reference to the death of Jesus. The voice
from heaven may refer to Jesus as the Servant of Yahweh by implicitly
citing Is 42:1 (see n. 69 below), but would first-century thought have
connected this passage with another Servant passage (Is 53) where suffering and death are described?

[42] For the lamb as the Suffering Servant see Anchor Bible, John, pp.
60–61.

that he must suffer and die. Scripture alone neither favors nor disproves a theory that posits a psychological development of Jesus' knowledge of what lay in store for him.

B. *Foreknowledge of the destruction of Jerusalem*

Another classical prophecy attributed to Jesus is that he predicted the destruction of Jerusalem. We have already discussed the prediction or threat about the destruction of the Temple; but this can scarcely be used as an example of successful prophecy, for it is in no way apparent how Jesus fulfilled the second part of the prediction about rebuilding the Temple in three days. The early Church had to reinterpret the saying in order to see a fulfillment (see note 37). Let us concentrate here on the prediction of the destruction of Jerusalem in the Synoptic eschatological discourse. This could be considered as a clear prophecy only in the Lucan wording. In Mk 13:14 Jesus speaks obscurely of the desolating sacrilege set up where it ought not to be. Mt 24:15 clarifies (correctly) by explaining that the "desolating sacrilege" is the one spoken of by Daniel the prophet (Dn 9:27, 12:11). Since Dn referred to the profanation of the Temple altar by Antiochus Epiphanes, Mt continues the explanation by identifying Mk's "where it ought not to be" as the holy place or Temple. Thus Mk and Mt agree in having Jesus figuratively predict a profanation of the Temple. But in Lk 21:20 Jesus says: "When you see Jerusalem surrounded by armies, then know that its desolation has come near." Some would see here a clear prediction of the Roman capture of Jerusalem in A.D. 70.

From a critical viewpoint many have suggested that Lk rewrote the earlier and vaguer prediction after the destruction of Jerusalem, and so we have a *vaticinium ex eventu*. But C. H. Dodd[43] has shown that such a suggestion is unnecessary. The Lucan description need not flow from a *post factum* knowledge of the tragedy of A.D 70; rather its vocabulary is that of the prophetic description of the fall of Jerusalem to the Babylonians in the sixth century B.C. Thus, while in Mk and Mt the prototype Jesus offers for the coming disaster stems from the havoc Antiochus Epiphanes wrought in Jerusalem, the prototype in Lk is a more ancient disaster. Yet even were the Lucan saying faithful to the original words of Jesus,[44] Dodd's very argument would imply that it is not a prophecy that demands exact knowledge of the future. Like Jeremiah and Ezekiel, Jesus would be threatening disaster to a rebellious Jerusalem,[45] and he would be using traditional language to do so. The saying would not indicate that he knew when or how this disaster would come about.

Another expression of Jesus' general conviction of impending disaster for Jerusalem can be found in his prediction that the great buildings of the Temple would be destroyed and that not one stone would be left upon another (Mk 13:2 and par.). If anyone would propose that this represented an exact foreknowledge of what would happen in A.D. 70, he need simply be reminded that the gigantic blocks of the Temple foundation are

[43] "The Fall of Jerusalem and the 'Abomination of Desolation,' " *Journal of Roman Studies* 37 (1947) 48–54.

[44] This cannot be taken for granted simply because the saying is not necessarily a *vaticinium ex eventu*.

[45] Jesus was not alone among his contemporaries in this premonition. There is a Jewish tradition (TalBab, *Gittin* 56a; Midrash Rabbah on Lam 1, 5; #31) that Rabbi Zadok began fasting about A.D. 30 to forestall the destruction of Jerusalem. Ca. A.D. 62 Jesus bar Ananias warned of the impending destruction of the Temple (Josephus, *War* VI 6, 3; #300 ff.).

still standing firmly one upon the other in Jerusalem.

Thus, in the two instances of Jesus' knowledge of the future that we have studied, the Gospel evidence when critically examined would demand no more than that Jesus would have had firm general convictions about the unrolling of God's plan in a way that would lead to death and victory for him and to punishment for Jerusalem. This type of conviction is characteristic of the Old Testament prophets. Neither in their case nor in Jesus' do we have really scientific proof for a detailed foreknowledge of unpredictable future events, a foreknowledge that could be given by God alone.

C. Foreknowledge of the Parousia

This aspect of Jesus' foreknowledge reflects in a different way on the total problem of whether and how his knowledge was limited. The instances dealt with above concerned predictions of things that actually happened; here we are concerned with the prediction of something that has not happened, and we must ask whether Jesus claimed to know when it would happen or mistakenly expected it to happen within a short time. We shall group here statements about the coming of the Son of Man, about the return of Jesus, and about the coming of the kingdom of God in power.[46] The divergence in these statements presents a very complicated situation that we cannot possibly hope to solve, but it will be very useful to classify the different temporal aspirations that seem to be involved in these statements.

[46] Such a grouping undoubtedly represents an oversimplification. The coming of God's kingdom would not necessarily include the coming of the Son of Man. Many Protestant exegetes who think that the references to the future coming of the Son of Man stem from Jesus hold that Jesus expected a Son of Man other than himself.

1. ANTICIPATIONS OF AN IMMEDIATE PAROUSIA

(a) *A Parousia during the ministry.* In Mt 10:23 Jesus instructs the Twelve to go to Israel and to preach (in the the parallel in Mk 6:7, 30 the scene is one of his sending them two by two into the towns of Galilee). Jesus warns them that they will meet persecution, but he assures them: "When they persecute you in one town, flee to the next; for truly, I assure you, you will not have gone through all the towns of Israel before the Son of Man comes." Combining the Matthean and Marcan versions, A. Schweitzer put forward his famous theory that Jesus expected the Parousia before the Twelve had finished their Galilean mission. When they returned without this having happened, disappointment brought Jesus to realize that his death would be necessary to bring about God's intervention. Today few would follow Schweitzer in this interpretation. The Matthean and Marcan scenes cannot be combined. The setting of Mt 10 (e.g., references to persecution by synagogues, governors, and kings in vv. 17–18) is that of the later Church; and in its present form at least, 10:23 must be understood in that atmosphere and not as a reference to an expectation within the ministry of Jesus. The Palestinian church is assuring itself that, despite persecution, it will not have exhausted all possibilities of preservation before the Son of Man comes.

(b) *A Parousia immediately after Jesus' death.* This seems to be the import of Jn 14:3 where Jesus says that he is departing but will return to take his disciples along with him. A comparison with 1 Th 4:16–17 suggests that Christians would have understood this return in terms of the Parousia. M. E. Boismard[47] has argued that 14:3 represents one of the oldest eschatological strains in Jn. An interpretation of a Parousia right after death might be placed on the words of Jesus to the high priest in Mk 14:62: "You will see the Son of Man sitting at the right hand of the Power and coming with the clouds of heaven."[48] Mk 14:25 and Lk 23:42–43 are other passages that would be most intelligible if Jesus expected immediate victory after death. All of this would fit in with a theory that Jesus did not know precisely what form his victory over death would take. One might conjecture that as a Jew he spoke of this victory in terms of the imagery of Dn and the coming of the Son of Man,[49] whereas it was the resurrection that took place after his death, and the Parousia remained in the future. One cannot refute scientifically the possibility of such a theory, nor can one prove it. All of the statements given above are capable of other interpretations, and no one of them specifies the precise moment of the coming of the Son of Man.

2. ANTICIPATIONS THAT IMPLY AN INTERVAL BETWEEN JESUS' DEATH AND THE PAROUSIA

This view is supported by many texts that never mention the Parousia; for an interval is implied by all refer-

[47] "L'évolution du thème eschatologique dans les traditions johanniques," Revue Biblique 68 (1961) 518–523.

[48] Mt 26:64 and Lk 22:69 (each in its own way) modify the verb in this saying with an adverbial phrase: "from now on." Lk omits the reference to the coming of the Son of Man, perhaps because the saying seemed to imply an immediate Parousia.

[49] To be exact, the New Testament expectation represents a modification of the literal sense of Dn where the Son of Man is not an individual so much as a symbolic figure, representing Israel or God's saints. In Dn the Son of Man is not depicted as coming to men but as coming to God.

ences to a church or a community life, a mission of the disciples to Israel or beyond; by the growth parables; by the orders to baptize and to commemorate Jesus in the Eucharist, etc.

(a) *A Parousia in the lifetime of Jesus' hearers.* There are two famous passages in Mk that support this:

— Mk 13:30 and par. "Truly, I assure you, this generation will not pass away before all these things take place." In the present context "these things" would have to include the coming of the Son of Man described in 13:26. But for an inquiry about the original meaning the present context has little value, for most scholars recognize that the eschatological discourse in Mk 13 is a collection of once independent sayings. A. Vögtle,[50] in the latest Catholic treatment of the logion, agrees with Taylor and a host of Protestant scholars that the original reference of "these things" was the destruction of the Temple mentioned in 13:2–4. All efforts to explain away the temporal limits of the saying by claiming that "this generation" refers to the existence of mankind are refuted, in my judgment, by the closely parallel saying we cite next.

— Mk 9:1 (Vulgate 8:31). "Truly, I assure you, there are some standing here who will not taste death before they see the kingdom of God come with power."[51] Mt 16:28 offers an interpretation of what Mk's last clause implies; it reads: " . . . before they see the Son of Man coming in his kingdom." In order to avoid the implication that the Parousia will take place while some of Jesus' hearers are alive, some scholars question Mt's interpretation and suggest that the saying does not refer to the Parousia, or

[50] *Art. cit.,* 642–647.
[51] The parallel in Lk 9:27 omits "with power," perhaps to make the prediction vaguer.

that it is inauthentic or a secondary rewriting of Mk 13:30 and referred originally to the destruction of the Temple (so Vögtle).

In addition to the Marcan tradition, there is some Johannine support for this early anticipation of the Parousia. This is of interest because the general Johannine tendency has been to reinterpret Parousia expectations in terms of realized eschatology.

— Jn 1:51: "Truly, I assure you, you will see the sky opened and the angels of God ascending and descending upon the Son of Man." This saying might have been listed among those that imply a Parousia during the ministry; but it is probably an independent saying, out of place in its present context,[52] and all that we can tell from it is that Jesus' *disciples* are promised a vision of the (seemingly) victorious Son of Man.

— Jn 21:22: "If it is my will that he [the Beloved Disciple] remain until I come, how does that concern you?" The obvious import of the saying is that Jesus will return during the Disciple's lifetime, and this is how Christians interpreted it (21:23). But since the Beloved Disciple was dying or dead, the Johannine author of Chap. 21 employs casuistry to show that Jesus' promise was not absolute.

If one accepts such logia without reinterpretation, one can be certain that neither of the Marcan sayings was a late creation; for from the 60's on, when the apostolic generation was dying out, such statements became a problem precisely because they were not fulfilled.[53] They are

---

[52] For detail see Anchor Bible John, pp. 88–91.

[53] The havoc that they caused at the end of the century is implicit in Jn 21 and explicit in 2 Pt 3:4 where scoffers use them to cast doubt on the Parousia.

either substantially *ipsissima verba* of Jesus or the composition of the first generation. One might theorize that the first generation, puzzled by the fact that the Parousia did not take place immediately, consoled itself by the assurance that the Parousia would at least come in its lifetime.[54] However, the reason that causes many scholars not to regard them as *ipsissima verba* or at least to claim that they were not originally a reference to the Parousia is the theological thesis that Jesus could not have been mistaken about the time of the Parousia which, de facto, did not take place during the lifetime of his hearers.

(b) *A Parousia delayed and preceded by apocalyptic signs.* These notions do not have to go together, but the mention of a great number of apocalyptic signs before the Parousia does give the impression that it is not coming too soon (see reasoning in 2 Th 2:3 ff.). The eschatological discourse in Mk 13, Mt 24–25, and Lk 21 lists the signs that will precede the coming of the Son of Man, e.g., false-Messiahs, persecution, war, and cosmic cataclysms. While these chapters open with the question of the destruction of the Temple, they discuss both the punishment of Jerusalem and the Parousia; and it is very difficult to interpret what the apocalyptic signs were originally meant to precede. Moreover, many would think that such sayings did not come from Jesus but from the Palestinian church, using the language of Jewish apocalyptic and seeking to console itself when the master did not return. There is also a group of sayings that specifically refer to

[54] For instance, the hint in Mk 9:1 that some will be dead when Jesus pared with the problem in 1 Th 4:13 ff. about those who died before the comes (it is stated that only "some" will not taste death) may be com- Parousia.

a delay of the Parousia without invoking apocalyptic, e.g., Mt 24:48; 25:5, 19.[55]

(c) A Parousia the time of which cannot be foretold. A group of sayings insists that the disciples cannot know when the Lord is coming — his coming will be like that of a thief in the night or the unexpected return of a master (Mt 24:42–44 = Lk 12:39–40; Mt 24:50 = Lk 12:46; Mt 25:13). Lk 17:20–21 is particularly interesting in the light of the references to apocalyptic signs cited above: "The kingdom of God is not coming with signs to be observed. . . . The kingdom of God is in the midst of you." Which is the more original strain in Jesus' teaching? Even more famous is Mk 13:32 which implies that Jesus himself did not know when all these things would come to pass: "Of that day or that hour no one knows, not even the angels in heaven, nor the Son, but only the Father." Some have questioned the authenticity of the saying because it is the only place in Mk where Jesus speaks of himself absolutely as "the Son," and indeed that might be a late feature. Others have thought that the early Church attributed the saying to Jesus to explain the seeming contradictions among his predictions. One is certain, however, that it ran against the grain of the Church to attribute ignorance to Jesus, and most authors would accept the saying as authentic.[56]

[55] We may add Lk 19:11 where Jesus corrects the belief of the disciples that the kingdom of God is to come immediately; also Lk 17:22 where Jesus speaks of an unfulfilled longing on the part of the disciples to see one of the days of the Son of Man.

[56] Lk does not report the Marcan saying; many mss. of Mt report the Matthean parallel (24:36) without the key phrase "nor the Son." Yet Haenchen, Weg Jesu, p. 452, thinks that only the later Church would have resisted such attribution of inferiority to Jesus; the earlier attitude is seen in 1 Cor 15:28 where Jesus is subjected to the Father. W. G. Kümmel, Promise and Fulfilment, Studies in Biblical Theology 13 (Naperville: Allenson, 1957) 42, cites a list of authors who accept Mk 13:32 as belonging to the oldest tradition, even though its wording has not

How can one establish the original outlook of Jesus amidst such a confusion of expectations? Undoubtedly, some of the confusion can reasonably be explained away. Seeming contradictions are often created by the microscopic analysis to which we subject Gospel passages, and at times they can be solved by common sense. It cannot be doubted that some of the confusion that now appears was caused by early Christians who reinterpreted Jesus' statements in the light of traditional eschatological expectations. In particular, it seems plausible that statements that once referred to the coming of the Son of Man in judgment on Jerusalem have been reinterpreted to refer to the Parousia in glory (so A. Feuillet,[57] and John A. T. Robinson). Yet, with all these allowances, one finds it difficult to believe that Jesus' own position was clear. The New Testament Epistles give independent evidence of the confusion that reigned in first-century thought about the Parousia;[58] and, *salvo meliore judicio*, such confusion could scarcely have arisen if Jesus both knew about the indefinite delay of the Parousia and expressed himself clearly on the subject.

Since it is not reasonable to suppose that he knew about the Parousia but for some mysterious reason expressed himself obscurely, one is almost forced to take at face value the admission of Mk 13:32 that Jesus did not know when the Parousia would take place.[59] Many

---

remained intact. In an earlier age, P. W. Schmiedel, in *Encyclopaedia Biblica* (New York: Macmillan, 1901) Vol. 2, col. 1881, listed Mk 13:32 as among the five "absolutely credible" general statements of the Gospel about Jesus.

[57] His article "Parousie," *VDBS* 6, cols. 1331–1419, is an important treatment with excellent bibliography.

[58] Compare 1 Th with 2 Th; 1 Cor 15 with 2 Cor 5; 1 Pt 4:7 with 2 Pt 3:4–11.

[59] Under Pope Vigilius in 553 (DBS 419) there was a condemnation of an error of Nestorianism which proposed that Jesus Christ, true Son

Catholics are willing to accept this today, but on this very basis they explain away the statements that attribute to Jesus the expectation of an immediate Parousia or of one within the lifetime of his disciples. B. Rigaux[60] distinguishes between what Jesus *taught* (namely, that he did not know the time of the Parousia) and what he *hoped* for in an apocalyptic setting (namely, a Parousia soon). Vögtle[61] rightly objects that the statements that refer to a Parousia within a short time are not especially apocalyptic and are clearly taught, e.g., they are preceded by "Truly, I assure you." Yet Vögtle himself manages to explain away by exegesis all reference to the Parousia in the promises of what will happen in the lifetime of Jesus' hearers. Is it totally inconceivable that, since Jesus did not know when the Parousia would occur, he tended to think and say that it would occur soon? Would not the inability to correct contemporary views on this question be the logical effect of ignorance?

That God would make Jesus victorious and would eventually establish His own reign was a basic conviction

of God and true Son of Man, was ignorant of future things and of the day of the Last Judgment and could have known such things only in so much as a deity dwelt in him as if in another individual. This error is so tied into the Nestorian theory of two persons or beings in Christ that its condemnation would really not affect the modern non-Nestorian problematic. Ca. 600 Pope Gregory (DBS 474–475) tended to interpret Mk 13:32 as an accommodation of God's Son to human speech. He maintained that the Son of God *in* his human nature knew the time of the Parousia, but this knowledge did not come *from* his human nature. This statement invokes theological distinctions that go beyond what we can determine from the exegesis of the passage; and so while it may be of importance to theologians dealing with the hypostatic union (it is scarcely a *de Fide* pronouncement), it does not really interpret the literal sense of the scriptural passage. We know of no Church statement that would forbid the interpretation of the literal sense of Mk 13:32 in the sense given above.

[60] "La seconde venue de Jésus," *La Venue du Messie* (*Recherches bibliques* 6; Desclée de Brouwer, 1962) p. 190.

[61] *Art. cit.*, 636 ff.

of Jesus' life and mission. Because there is evidence, nay even a statement, that Jesus did not know when the ultimate victory would take place, many Catholic theologians would propose that such knowledge was not an essential of Jesus' mission. Could theologians then also admit that Jesus was not protected from the confused views of his era about the time of the Parousia? An exegete cannot solve such a question; he can only point out the undeniable confusion in the statements attributed to Jesus.

IV. JESUS' UNDERSTANDING OF HIMSELF AND OF HIS MISSION

We come now to the most sensitive of all areas — an area with theological repercussions for the understanding of the hypostatic union and an area where the Church has shown herself consistently opposed to a minimalist solution. The modern biblical discussions in this area have centered on the titles of Christ (whether he himself claimed to be the Messiah, the Son of Man, the Son of God, God, etc.). In this essay we cannot attempt even to summarize what has been written on these subjects. Practicality demands that we be selective; and so we have chosen one title, "Messiah," that might be a key to Jesus' knowledge of his salvific mission to men, and another title, "Son of God," that might be a key to Jesus' knowledge of his relationship to Yahweh.

A. Jesus as the Messiah

There are two questions that we must keep distinct: (1) In what way did the early Christians accept Jesus as the Messiah? (2) When and/or to what extent did Jesus think of himself as the Messiah?

1. There is no doubt that the early Church confessed Jesus as the Messiah. A Christian was one who accepted Jesus as Messiah, and so popular was this designation of Jesus that "Christ" became part of his name. Yet within the New Testament there are conflicting indications as to what facet of Jesus' career brought men to confess him as Messiah. One is tempted to take these indications and to arrange them so that New Testament christology develops from earlier inadequate concepts to later adequate concepts. Yet, while one may suspect that certain christologies are more primitive than others, we cannot be certain of a sequence, nor that adequate and inadequate views did not originate at the same time. (The very use of the term "adequate" reflects the judgment of later orthodoxy.)

There are two christologies best attested in the kerygmatic sermons that Acts dates to the early days of the Church; and so for external as well as internal reasons these christologies are considered primitive.[62] According to Acts 3:20-21, when Jesus comes back from heaven in the Parousia, he will be the appointed Messiah sent by God. The earthly ministry of Jesus was only a preparation for his coming as the Messiah expected in Jewish thought, i.e., a Messiah coming to earth in power and glory. The future moment in which Jesus will appear is described as the time when there will be established "all that God spoke by the mouth of His prophets from of old." This has been called the oldest christology in

[62] See John A. T. Robinson, "The Most Primitive Christology of All?" *Journal of Theological Studies* 7 (1956) 177–189; also in *Twelve New Testament Studies, Studies in Biblical Theology* 34 (London: SCM, 1962).

the New Testament, for it implies virtually no change from the best-established late Jewish expectations of the Messiah. The other christology is voiced in Acts 2:36 (cf. also 5:31) which says that it is the risen-ascended Jesus whom God has made Messiah. God seated the risen Jesus at His right hand, and this glorification made him Messiah. Here we have a partial modification of the Jewish concept: the Messiah remains a glorious, victorious figure, but his reign is in heaven, not on earth.

In the christology of the Gospels Jesus is seen as Messiah during his public ministry. The classical text for this appears in the Synoptic scene of Peter's confession (Mk 8:29 and par.). It is interesting to note, however, that the Johannine form of this scene (6:69) does not mention Messiah but "the Holy One of God"; the Johannine confession of Jesus as the Messiah occurs when Andrew speaks to Peter (1:41; also 11:27). Such christology required a radical reinterpretation of the Jewish concept of Messiah, a reinterpretation in terms of a suffering figure. This is implied in the relationship between the messianic confession in Mk 8:29 and the first of the predictions of the passion, death, and resurrection of the Son of Man in 8:31.

All of the messianic theories thus far mentioned allow of (or, in the case of the first two, imply) an adoptionist interpretation — there was a time when Jesus was not the Messiah; he became or would become Messiah. Adoptionism is ruled out in the infancy narratives of Mt and Lk where it is proposed that Jesus was the Messiah from the time of his incarnation.[63] Obviously here we are moving toward a divine Messiah.

[63] In Mt 1:23; 2:6 and Lk 1:31–33 messianic passages are cited, i.e., passages that seemingly were being interpreted messianically in Jesus' time.

This diversity of early Christian views would, a priori, make one think that Jesus himself did not make lucidly affirmative messianic claims during his ministry. The standard explanation, however, has been that his lucid claims were not understood because of the obtuseness or hardness of heart of his hearers. It is suggested that it took time for the Jewish presuppositions about the Messiah to be modified and tailored to suit Jesus' career, so that men could recognize him as Messiah.

2. When we turn to the question of Jesus' thought about himself as the Messiah, we are in an area for which Scripture gives us little evidence. Even if the infancy narratives are accepted at face value, they do not directly answer the question of whether the young Jesus (in the womb [!], as an infant, or after the age of reason) thought of himself as the Messiah. If we turn to the Gospel accounts of the ministry, a frequently proposed, sophisticated thesis is that Jesus' baptism revealed to him that he was the Messiah.[64] However, such a thesis faces two formidable objections from modern biblical science.

First, the thesis presupposes that Jesus did accept Messiah as a designation for himself. Often in Catholic circles it is not sufficiently emphasized that in the oldest tradition of Peter's confession (Mk 8:29; Lk 9:20)[65] Jesus

[64] Some non-Catholics would resuscitate adoptionism and speak of Jesus' becoming Messiah at his baptism. For Catholics Pope Pius X (DBS 3435) condemned the Modernist proposition that Christ had not always been conscious of his messianic dignity. The theological note to be attached to this type of condemnation is notoriously difficult to determine. Moreover, the idea is condemned in the whole context of Modernist historicism where it served as a denial of Jesus' divinity. Would the idea be condemned when held by a theologian who interprets it in a way that does not conflict with the dogma of Nicaea? Some do not appreciate that the Catholic theologians who are discussing this today are doing so not from any disloyalty to the Church's dogma but precisely from a desire to clarify Christian thought.

[65] In Mt 16:18 there is an additional confession to Jesus as "the Son of the living God." To the combined confession Jesus reacts positively.

did not affirm Peter's estimate of him as the Messiah, but ordered silence[66] and spoke of suffering.

To the point-blank question of the high priest, "Are you the Messiah?" Jesus answers in a qualified manner, "You have said so."[67] This probably means that, while Jesus will not refuse the title and thus deny his unique role before the high priest, nevertheless, the phraseology is not what he would spontaneously choose and he is not happy about its implications. At any rate, Jesus is depicted as answering the high priest, not by quoting a passage about the Messiah but by quoting a passage about the Son of Man.

Only in one instance in the Gospels does Jesus accept the title of Messiah without reservation (Jn 4:25–26). Even if one accepts this dialogue between Jesus and the Samaritan woman as straight historical material (an assumption not to be made lightly in peculiarly Johannine material), one must recognize that he is accepting a Samaritan concept of Messiahship, which was apparently

Many Catholic scholars now regard Mt's scene as composite, suggesting that Mt has joined to Mk's account another (perhaps post-resurrectional) confession by Peter. For bibliography and for the proof of the orthodoxy of this view see my New Testament Essays (Milwaukee: Bruce, 1965), p. 208, n. 37.

[66] This touches on the question of the Marcan Secret (Taylor, op. cit., pp. 122–124) wherein Jesus is presented as keeping his Messiahship secret during his ministry. Is this a theological invention (Wrede)? Did Jesus keep quiet for political reasons? Or was it because his notions of Messiahship differed from those of his contemporaries (Taylor)? A variant of the latter view is that there was so much difference that he never fully accepted the title of Messiah.

[67] So Mt 26:64. (In Lk 22:67 Jesus answers ambiguously, "If I tell you, you will not believe"; the same type of answer is found independently in Jn 10:24–25.) In Mk 14:62 Jesus answers with an unconditional "I am." Scholars who think that Mk always has an earlier tradition tend to interpret Mt's "You have said so" as an unconditional affirmative. However, the very similar answer to Pilate in Jn 18:37 offers support for the interpretation we have given above. Christological development in the primitive Church would suggest that the vague answer is older than the clear affirmative.

less nationalistic than the Jewish concept.[68] In Mt 23:10
Jesus indirectly identifies himself as the Messiah: he instructs the disciples that they are not to be called masters,
for they have one master, the Messiah (= Jesus, presumably). This passage appears only in Mt, and the situation envisaged seems to be that of the later Church. One
would be hard put to defend this saying as the unvarnished
ipsissima verba of Jesus.

It is possible that this consideration of the problems
in the individual passages does not do justice to the
totality of the evidence and that more emphasis should
be put on the argument that Jesus would not have been
so universally acclaimed as Messiah in the early Church
if he had been so wary of the title. Nevertheless, at least
an intelligent case can be made out for the thesis that
Jesus never really accepted Messiah as a correct or adequate
designation for his role, even though he would not cate-
gorically refuse the title (see also note 25).

Second, the thesis is objectionable because it is impossible from the biblical accounts to tell whether the
baptism revealed anything at all to Jesus. The speculation
behind the thesis is that Jesus came to John the Baptist
as one among a crowd, not knowing himself to be different
from the others or, at least, not knowing in what way
he was different. At the baptism he was told by God:
"You are my beloved Son; with you I am well pleased,"
and thus he learned that he was the Messiah.[69] The diffi-

[68] See Anchor Bible *John*, pp. 172–173.

[69] The words spoken from heaven are predominantly an echo of a
Servant passage of Deutero-Isaiah (42:1), with perhaps an admixture of
Gn 22:2. But perhaps they also echo Ps 2:7 ("You are my son; this day
I have begotten you"), a psalm that seemingly received messianic inter-
pretation in Jesus' time. The reference to the psalm would be clearer in
Mk 1:11 and Lk 3:22 than in Mt 3:17 ("This is my beloved Son").
There is an interesting variant of Lk 3:22 that cites Ps 2:7 word for
word. Although textual criticism does not favor the variant, many com-

culty of establishing scientifically the historical character of a theophany is enormous; but placing that aside, let us ask whether the thesis of a revelation to Jesus corresponds with the intent of the narratives. Certainly it does not correspond with that of Mt and Lk, for the existence of infancy narratives in these Gospels means that the two evangelists did not think of the baptism as a first revelation to Jesus.[70] One may argue that in Mk the situation is different; and also in Mk (alone) both the vision and the voice in the baptismal scene are directed to Jesus.[71] Yet the variance between Mk and the other Gospels on the latter point is not really meaningful, for the scene is not directed to Jesus but to the Christian reader of the Gospel.[72] It is designed to tell him at the beginning of the Gospel and on the highest authority who Jesus is, namely, the Messiah (see note 69), and the Servant of Yahweh, and God's own Son. D. E. Nineham[73] has summed up the situation admirably: "He [Mark] makes

mentators have argued for its originality on theological grounds: it was too adoptionistic and was changed to the safer reading found in most mss.

[70] See Lk 2:49. Also Mt 3:14–15 has a scene that depicts Jesus as quite aware of special status.

[71] In Mt the vision is directed to Jesus, but the voice speaks of him in the third person. In Lk the voice is directed to Jesus, but a wider audience is implied for the vision (since the Holy Spirit is in "a bodily form"). In Jn 1:32–34 the voice and the vision are reported by John the Baptist.

[72] E. Haenchen, Der Weg Jesu (Berlin: Töpelmann, 1966) p. 61. "The account [Mk] does not wish to describe an inner experience of Jesus (for that would be something far from the evangelist's mind) but to tell the reader who Jesus really is." In firmly rejecting the idea that the baptismal vision was the call of Jesus, he rightly characterizes this as a thesis springing from the Protestant Liberalism at the beginning of the century (e.g. J. Weiss). It is embarrassing that popular Catholic writers are now suddenly discovering and espousing such theses on the assumption that they represent the latest in biblical exegesis. A more serious Catholic study along these lines by A. Nisin (Histoire de Jésus) is refuted by Vögtle, art. cit., p. 658 ff.

[73] St. Mark in the Pelican Gospel Commentaries (London: Pelican, 1963) p. 58.

no attempt, for example, to say what effect these events had on Jesus himself; did they, for example, constitute a 'call' or a sudden revelation about himself, or only a confirmation of views he had already formed about himself? On the basis of St. Mark's account it is impossible to be sure and even idle to speculate."

To sum up the question of Jesus as the Messiah, it is dubious whether we should speak in any strict sense of "messianic" knowledge on Jesus' part since he may never have really identified his role as that of the Messiah. (We are not denying, of course, the existence of a more basic problem that one often speaks of as "messianic" consciousness: Jesus' consciousness of himself as the unique salvific agent — see below.) Moreover, any attempt to trace a beginning or development of "messianic" claim runs afoul of the complete lack of evidence for this type of speculation.

B.   *Jesus as the Son of God*

Often theologians prefer to study the problem of Jesus' knowledge of his divinity in terms of the question: "Did Jesus know he was God?" From a biblical viewpoint this question is so badly phrased that it cannot be answered and should not be posed. The New Testament does call Jesus "God,"[74] but this is a development of the later New Testament books. In the Gospels Jesus never uses the title "God" of himself; indeed in Mk 10:18 (a text that is almost certainly a genuine saying of Jesus) he refuses to be given a mark of respect that belongs to God alone. There are many passages in the New Testament writings that distinguish between God and Jesus. We do not mean

[74] Chapter One above gives the evidence supporting these statements.

that such passages prove that Jesus was not God; rather they reflect the terminological problem in the question that we are asking. For the Jew "God" meant God the Father in heaven; and to apply this term to Jesus who was not the Father and who had come down to earth made no sense. Later, precisely under the necessity of giving proper honor to Jesus, especially in the liturgy, it was understood that "God" was a broader term that could include both the Father and Jesus. This designation became more frequent for Jesus in the last third of the first century, as far as our evidence permits us to determine.

Therefore, when we ask whether during his ministry Jesus, a Palestinian Jew, knew that he was God, we are asking whether he identified himself and the Father — and, of course, he did not. Undoubtedly, some would wish to attribute to Jesus an anticipated understanding of the later broadness of the term "God" (or, indeed, even expect him to speak in trinitarian terminology), but can serious scholars simply presume that Jesus could speak and think in the vocabulary and philosophy of later times? And does one ignore a text like Mk 10:18?

In a biblical framework it is preferable to discuss the question of Jesus' divinity in terms of his claiming to be the unique Son of God. That the early Church confessed Jesus as the Son of God is admitted by all, and this confession may be quite ancient (see 1 Th 1:10 and Acts 9:20).[75] Does it have its roots in the way Jesus described himself? To prevent confusion, it is well to remind ourselves that "son of God" is a somewhat ambiguous term, for often it does not mean real divine filiation but only a special relationship to God (e.g., the Old

[75] Bultmann would attribute the confession of Jesus as Son of God to the Hellenistic Church; however, Cullmann, *Christology*, p. 275 ff. makes a strong case for Palestinian origin.

Testament use of the term for angels, the king, and the nation of Israel). In particular, in the New Testament it appears as a messianic designation, flowing from its use in the Old Testament for the king;[76] such a usage would come under our previous discussion of Jesus as Messiah.

For our purposes the question "Did Jesus consider himself the Son of God?" must refer to a unique sonship that is not shared by ordinary men. To support an affirmative answer to the question it has been customary to argue that Jesus spoke of God as "my Father" and that he never joined himself to others in speaking of "our Father." The argument is not without weakness. First of all, the expression "my Father" never appears in Mk; it appears only four times in Lk; the frequent usage is a Matthean feature, and for not a single one of the Matthean usages of "my Father" is there a Synoptic parallel.[77] Moreover, if in Mt Jesus speaks of "my Father," he also speaks frequently to his disciples of "your Father."[78] What right has the exegete to assume that "my Father" implies a more intimate relationship to God than "your Father"

[76] There is no published, pre-Christian Jewish evidence for "son of God" as a title for the Davidic Messiah. Yet it is quite logical that such a designation may have been prompted by the messianic interpretation of Ps 2 where God was thought to address the Messiah as "my son." For New Testament instances where "son of God" may be a messianic designation notice the conjunction of Messiah and son of God in Mt 16:16; 26:63; Jn 20:31, although one cannot be sure tha' in the mind of the evangelist the term "son of God" had not taken on deeper meaning. The latter is probably the case with Mt 16:16. In the two statements of the angel in Lk 1:32–35, the first one implicitly identifies Jesus as the Messiah, and the second calls him the "son of God."

[77] It is instructive to compare Mt 12:50 ("the will of my Father") with Mk 3:35 and Lk 8:20 ("the will [or word] of God"), and to compare Mt 26:29 ("my Father's kingdom") with Mk 14:25 ("kingdom of God").

[78] A whole group of passages in the Sermon on the Mount teach the disciples to think of God as their Father in a very special way (Mt 5:16, 45, 48, etc.). In Mt 7:21 Jesus speaks of the will of "my Father"; in 18:14 he speaks of the will of "your Father."

implies? J. Jeremias[79] has argued eloquently that Jesus'
custom of addressing God as "Abba" ("Father") in prayer
is distinctive; the Aramaic word is a caritative (= "Daddy")
and implies familiar, family relationship.[80] Since this is
undoubtedly one of the *ipsissima verba* of Jesus, one must
admit that Jesus claimed a special relationship to God as
his Father beyond the general relationship postulated in
contemporary Judaism. But Jesus offered to share this
relationship with his followers: he taught them to pray
to God as "Abba" (Lk 11:2, the original form of the
address in the Lord's Prayer[81]) and they carried this custom even into the Greek-speaking world (Gal 4:6; Rom
8:15). The Johannine tradition also implies a sharing of
sonship, for the Prologue (1:12) speaks of all who believe
in Jesus' name becoming children of God. In Jn 20:17
the risen Jesus says: "I am ascending to my Father and
your Father." Drawing on the analogy of a similar phrase
in Ruth 1:16, F.-M. Catharinet[82] has shown that Jesus
means "my Father who is now your Father" — through
the post-resurrectional gift of the Spirit God becomes the
Father of those who believe in Jesus. Now some of the
New Testament theologians carefully distinguished between the type of sonship that Jesus communicated to
those who believed in him and Jesus' own divine sonship
that was unique.[83] Yet it is not easy to prove scientifically

[79] "Abba," *The Central Message of the New Testament* (London:
SCM, 1965), pp. 9–30. For some important examples of "Abba" or
"Father" see Mk 14:36; Lk 23:34.

[80] *Abba* may mean "my Father"; if it does, then the Matthean practice
of using "my Father" may reflect an authentic custom of Jesus.

[81] See R. E. Brown, *New Testament Essays*, "The Pater Noster as an
Eschatological Prayer," pp. 217–253.

[82] See above, Chapter One, n. 13.

[83] John confines the word *huios*, "son," to Jesus and speaks of Christians
as God's *tekna*, "children." Paul (Gal 4:5; Rom 8:15) attributes to
Christians a type of adoptive sonship.

that such a distinction existed in Jesus' own words and promises. At least, however, one may suspect that if Jesus presented himself as the first of many to stand in a new and special relationship to God as Father, that very claim implies that his sonship was in some way superior to the sonship of all who would follow him.

Perhaps the proof we seek can be found if we turn from the passages where Jesus speaks of God as Father to the passages where he speaks of himself as Son. Are there any instances in the Synoptic accounts of the ministry where Jesus speaks of himself absolutely as "*the* Son" of God? There is one instance in the "Q" tradition and one instance in Mk. The former is the famous "Johannine" logion shared by Mt 11:27 and Lk 10:22: "No one knows the Son except the Father, and no one knows the Father except the Son and anyone to whom the Son chooses to reveal Him." This saying, so Johannine in style, has many Semitic features and could well be an adapted form of an original saying of Jesus. We say "adapted" because J. Jeremias[84] has made a very convincing suggestion that the original was parabolic in style. Jesus is drawing on the maxim that a father and son know each other intimately and a son is the best one to reveal the innermost thoughts of the father. In this case, the definite article before "Son" is the definite article of parabolic style indicating a generic situation, e.g., "The sower went out to sow seed." English tends to use an indefinite article in such a situation, but the definite form is good Aramaic. This suggestion makes us wary of assuming that Jesus meant to describe himself as "the Son" in an absolute sense (although that is not excluded since many of the

84 "Abba," pp. 23–25.

parables have allegorical features as well, and Jesus could be playing on his being "*the* Son").

The other saying is Mk 13:32: "Of that day or that hour no one knows, not even the angels in heaven, nor the Son, but only the Father." It is curious that the very passage that speaks of Jesus absolutely as the Son of God is the most famous passage in the Gospels for indicating that Jesus' knowledge was limited! We discussed this passage above and saw that it is not without difficulty. Another Synoptic passage that is thought to claim unique sonship for Jesus occurs in the Parable of the Vinedressers. There the son (= Jesus) who is finally sent to collect the rent, only to be killed, is designated as "uniquely beloved" (agapētos) in Mk 12:6 and Lk 20:13. Although the indirectness of the description of Jesus is a difficulty, the fact that agapētos tends to be used for an only son would make this an extremely important passage were not agapētos missing from the Matthean form of the parable (21:37). The form without agapētos may well be original, for it is easier to posit an addition by the other traditions than an omission by Mt.

To sum up, the way in which Jesus speaks of God as Father certainly indicates that he claimed a special relationship to God. But it remains difficult to find in the Synoptic account of the public ministry an incontrovertible proof that he claimed a unique sonship that other men could not share. However, it may well be here that the quest for absolutely scientific proof causes us to miss the woods for the trees. One could argue for a convergence of probabilities that Jesus did claim to be God's unique Son. It is when we stand before such a question that we realize the frustrating limitations imposed on research by the nature of the material we work with — material magnificently illuminated by post-resurrectional faith, but for that very reason far from ideal for scientific study.

And just this difficulty has forced us to ignore two bodies of Gospel material which, if taken at face value, could settle the question of whether Jesus claimed a unique divine sonship. There is absolutely no doubt that the Jesus of the fourth Gospel claims to be God's Son who alone has seen and heard God and who has come to earth to reveal God to man. He even describes himself as God's "only Son."[85] The present writer believes strongly that there is a core of historical material in the fourth Gospel, but he also recognizes that this material has been rethought in the light of late first-century theology. The Gospel was written to prove that Jesus is the Son of God (20:31), and the evangelist accomplishes this by letting Jesus speak as he is now in glory. The words may often be the words of Jesus of the ministry, but they are suffused with the glory of the risen Jesus. The use of Jn to determine scientifically how much Jesus knew of himself during his lifetime is far more difficult than the use of the other Gospels.

The second body of material to which we refer consists of the two independent infancy narratives of Mt and Lk. These agree that Jesus is God's Son in a unique manner, for God Himself begot Jesus. The virgin birth reflects indirectly on Jesus' knowledge of his sonship, for in the scheme of these two Gospels one could scarcely imagine

[85] Jn 3:16: monogenēs — that this does not mean "only-begotten" see D. Moody, *Journal of Biblical Literature* 72 (1953) 213–219. Jn is also the source of many statements that spring to mind when one asks about Jesus' consciousness of divinity, e.g.: "Before Abraham even came into existence, I AM" (8:58); "The Father and I are one" (10:30); "Whoever has seen me has seen the Father" (14:9). In Jn even the general audience of the ministry perceives that the claims that Jesus makes are tantamount to asserting that he is God (5:18; 10:33). For a detailed discussion of such statements the writer must refer the reader to the Anchor Bible *John*. Also see above, Chapter One, n. 52.

that Mary would not have told Jesus of the divine paternity (or of his Messiahship). Despite the fact that there are undoubtedly some very old Semitic elements in these infancy narratives, most non-Catholic critics do not consider them seriously as sources for the life of Jesus; and there are conflicts between the infancy narratives and the Gospel accounts of the ministry.[86] There has been little in the way of truly critical Catholic study of these narratives;[87] and until that has been done, Catholic scholarship is hampered in judging how much they can contribute to a scientific solution of the problem under consideration.

C. A better approach to the problem?

Before we close this discussion of Jesus' understanding of himself, we should like to suggest some very important distinctions, one theological and one exegetical, that may supply a key to the whole problem.

First, in the theological field. Often a certain confusion is introduced into the discussion of this topic by the equation of consciousness and knowledge. The question "Did Jesus identify himself as Messiah?" is described as the question of Jesus' messianic self-consciousness. Yet consciousness is not always the same as express knowledge; and while a study of the Messiah passages in the Gospels

[86] In the Lucan narrative John the Baptist is a close relative of Jesus; yet at the baptismal scene and later John the Baptist seems to have no knowledge of Jesus (Jn 1:31; Mt 11:2–3). All Jerusalem is aroused when the news comes that a star has announced the birth of the messianic king of the Jews at Bethlehem (Mt 2:3); yet later on at Jerusalem no one seems to remember this (Jn 7:41–42).

[87] In part this omission may have been caused by apprehension about how critical work on the infancy narratives would be received. The late J. Steinmann's cavalier dismissal of them won his Vie de Jésus (Paris: Denoël, 1959) the dubious distinction of being the last book (ever?) to be placed on the Index. Catholic study would be important in this area precisely because dogmas, e.g. the virginity of Mary, are involved.

may tell us whether or not Jesus expressed himself in terms of Messiahship, this study need not necessarily tell us much about his self-consciousness. Without embarking on a psychological discussion, perhaps we may say that consciousness is often an intuitive awareness and thus is distinct from an ability to express by formulating concepts and words, which is generally what people mean when they speak of knowledge. In human experience, especially in artistic matters or in one's awareness of oneself, there may be a lag between consciousness and express knowledge — one may be vividly conscious of something long before one finds a reasonably adequate way to express that consciousness.

Of the two titles we have discussed, we chose "Messiah" because it was an early formulation for describing Jesus in his salvific mission to men. Now we have seen that in the Gospels there is insufficient evidence that Jesus claimed the title or that he fully accepted it when it was offered to him. But this would not necessarily imply that he had no consciousness of a salvific mission to men (the type of mission that the Church called Messiahship when it had reinterpreted that term in a spiritual way). It could simply mean that he found Messiahship, as the term was understood in his time, an inadequate way to give expression to the mission of which he was conscious. One might ask about other titles given to Jesus by the Church, e.g., Suffering Servant or Savior. Again scholars would argue whether or not Jesus himself ever formulated his mission in such terms; but even if one thought that Jesus did not use such formulations, the question of his consciousness of a mission would not be solved.

If we turn to the title "Son of God," the question of Jesus' consciousness of a special relationship to God is not solved negatively if we cannot prove in a fully scientific manner that he claimed to be the unique Son of God. In the judgment of the later Church, "Son" was accepted as a reasonably adequate image through which to describe Jesus' relationship to Yahweh, but it is *possible* that in his lifetime Jesus never came to full use of this image. Still this does not necessarily mean that he was not conscious of the reality behind the relationship we call Sonship. In scholastic terminology concepts like "Son" and "Messiah" are the products of the intellect, and man is said to come into the world with an intellect that is a *tabula rasa*. Against Apollinarianism the Church maintained that Jesus had a human soul and thus a human intellect (*DBS* 146). Can theology admit that this intellect was also a *tabula rasa*, activated not by infused knowledge but by human experiences, as are other men's intellects? In this case it would have taken Jesus time to formulate concepts, and he might have found some of the concepts of his day inadequate to express what he wanted to say. One would then be able to say that his *knowledge* was limited, but such limitation would not at all exclude an intuitive *consciousness* of a unique relationship to God and of a unique mission to men.[88] The struggle of his life could have been one of finding the concepts and the words to express that relationship and that mission. Proving such a theory obviously goes far beyond the task and the capabilities of exegesis. For the most part exegesis can explore only the end product, i.e., the formulation and words used

[88] We objected above to the question "Did Jesus know he was God?" on the grounds that it does not take into account the semantic problem of what "God" meant in Jesus' time (= the Father). It is also objectionable because of the ambiguity possible in the word "know" — one must ask if the questioner is speaking about intuitive consciousness of divinity or express knowledge which involves the ability to find a meaningful formulation of consciousness.

by Jesus. But we do wish to insist that if exegesis gives us a picture of rather limited formulations, one should not jump to conclusions about consciousness.

Second, in the field of exegesis. Since formulation is to some extent reflective of consciousness, perhaps, if Messiahship and Sonship have not proved sufficiently fruitful fields of investigation, we are not approaching the problem of formulation correctly.[89] These titles were certainly popular in the early Church; yet our precise difficulty is that there are relatively few passages in the oldest Synoptic tradition wherein Jesus could be considered to accept the title of Messiah or to describe himself as the unique Son of God. Suppose that instead of starting out with a prefabricated question, we begin by studying the most ancient Gospel traditions to see how Jesus does describe his mission and his relationship to God. There we might have sufficient formulation to tell us something about his consciousness of himself.

I do not plan here to go into great detail, but it seems that an irreducible historical minimum in the Gospel presentation of Jesus is that he claimed to be the unique agent in the process of establishing God's kingship over

---

[89] H. Riesenfeld, "Observations on the Question of the Self-Consciousness of Jesus," *Svensk Exegetisk Arsbok* 25 (1960) 23–36, has some very interesting comments along this line of thought. "It is impossible to avoid the impression that the exegetical debate on the question of Jesus' self-consciousness has in the last decades moved too much on traditional lines" (24). "None of the prominent New Testament scholars of our generation . . . has been able to present a picture of the person of Jesus which succeeds in doing justice to the central figure of what is by far the most powerful spiritual movement in world history" (26). "May there not be a flaw in a too onesided analytical method? . . . It is no doubt the dimension of depth which is missing; that plasticity and 'form' which alone gives intelligibility — and above all 'life' — to a personality, to his thoughts and his work" (27). "The existence of the Gospels and, furthermore, the existence of the figure of Jesus in the Gospels, cannot be explained without the conditions created by Jesus, as a living, working and willing personality" (31).

men. He proclaimed that in *his* preaching and through *his* deeds God's kingship over men was making itself felt. From the beginning of Jesus' ministry to the end he exhibited unshakable confidence that he could authoritatively interpret the demands that God's kingship puts on men who are subject to it. We have seen above that when Jesus spoke of the next life or of the signs of the last times, he seems to have repeated the descriptions current in his time; but when he spoke of God's rule over men, he spoke with startling originality. This was his métier, and here he brooked no opposition. He could and did declare sins forgiven, modify the Law of Moses, violate the Sabbath ordinances, offend against the proprieties (eat with tax collectors and sinners), make stringent demands (forbid divorce; challenge to celibacy and to leave family ties), defy common sense (encouragement to turn the other cheek) — in short, teach as no teacher of his time taught. And if one allows that he worked miracles — an allowance that has sound exegetical backing, no matter how much it offends liberal philosophical presuppositions — then what he did in the interests of the kingship of God was also astonishing, for he acted against evil with a power that went far beyond the range of ordinary experience.

All of this certainly implies a consciousness of a unique ministry to men. Among the holy men of Israel's past one may find parallels to Jesus as regards individual sayings or deeds (Jeremiah, Elijah), but the total picture of Jesus breaks the mold. Moreover, the certainty with which Jesus spoke and acted implies a consciousness of a unique relationship to God. We have seen above that his conviction about the ultimate success of his mission (*perhaps* accompanied by a lack of knowledge about just how that victory would be achieved) resembles to some extent the conviction of the Old Testament prophets. But no prophet broke with the hallowed past in so radical a way and with so much assurance as did Jesus. The Gospel traditions agree in depicting him as a man who thinks he can act and speak for God.

Thus, while a scientific study may point out many limitations in the manner of expression attributed to Jesus in the most reliable Gospel material, such a study also portrays a man who defied ordinary limits in his claim to be the unique agent for establishing God's kingly rule. And in considering this very important evidence for Jesus' consciousness of himself, we should emphasize that there is no indication in the Gospels of a development of Jesus' basic conviction. From the very beginning of his ministry he proclaimed the kingdom of God, and finally he was crucified on a charge growing out of that proclamation. Perhaps the time when he would begin to preach was determined by the baptismal scene. Perhaps the place and the emphasis of his preaching were determined by considerations stemming from the social and political structures of his time (e.g., a ministry outside of Herod's territory after Herod's action against John the Baptist). Perhaps (and this is a much more problematic assumption) he did not foresee in detail the way in which the kingship of God would be established. But there is not the slightest evidence that his own role in the kingdom had to be revealed to him.[90] So far as Scripture is concerned, the awareness or

[90] Vögtle, art. cit., p. 662, makes a good point against those who treat the baptismal scene as a revelation to Jesus. The really new aspect of Jesus' preaching about the kingdom was not his prediction that it would come in power at some future date with the Parousia, but his contention that God's rule was active here and now in his own ministry without apocalyptic signs. Jewish thought had not prepared men to see the fulfillment of God's promises in one who walked the earth without royal political power, one who had not come on the clouds of heaven. What in the baptismal vision would have revealed to Jesus such a novel understanding of the kingdom?

consciousness that God's rule over men would be estab-
tablished through him *could have* sprung from his innermost being, for the first moment he speaks, he has this
consciousness.

V. CONCLUSION

As we close, we must once more stress the limits of our
discussion. This is a very short treatment of a very large
subject, and there is much more that should be said. The
evaluation of the biblical evidence represents one man's
opinion, limited by his abilities as a scholar and open to
challenge. But most important of all, the evaluation of
the Gospel evidence given above *does not predetermine
the theological interpretation to be drawn from it.*

Some theologians are convinced that, because of the
hypostatic union or because of special enlightenment given
to him by the beatific vision and/or infusion, Jesus could
not have been limited in what he knew, at least in matters
of religion, matters of the future, and matters regarding
himself. If a scriptural investigation points up the limitations in Jesus' statements about such matters, these theologians can simply say that, while Jesus actually knew what
was correct and what would happen, he adapted himself
to the circumstances of his time. His knowledge of the
Bible was perfect, but he conformed to the hermeneutics
of his time because it suited his purpose. He was perfectly
capable of phrasing exact statements about his divinity
but avoided doing so lest he cause scandal.

Other theologians will argue that neither the hypostatic
union nor other possible privileges extended to the God-
man necessarily endowed him with extraordinary knowledge in the matters just mentioned. They tend to attribute

to Jesus some sort of intuition or immediate awareness of what he was,[91] but they recognize that the ability to express this in a communicable way had to be acquired gradually. Thus they distinguish between two forms of knowledge (or, as has been suggested above, between self-consciousness and expressible knowledge). These theologians would have no difficulty at all in accepting at face value the limitations of knowledge that scientific biblical criticism finds in Jesus' statements. For them, whatever ignorance is implied in such statements is real rather than feigned, as it was for the first group of theologians. The exegete has no means to solve such a dispute, even though most modern Catholic exegetes would be far more at home with the second theological solution than with the first.

As a final comment on our discussion, let me insist that the evaluation of the Gospel evidence given above, if correct, does nothing to detract from the dignity of Jesus. The whole discussion has been predicated on an acceptance of him as "true God of true God." If in the Gospel reports his knowledge seems to have been limited, such limitation would simply show to what depths divine condescension went in the incarnation — it would show just how human was the humanity of Jesus. Perhaps there is a danger, however, that such a presentation as we have given may cause a generation already prone to reject authority to object

[91] See articles cited in n. 2. Durand speaks of the pure knowledge acquired by the beatific vision, knowledge that is aconceptual and non-abstractive, knowledge not employing signs of which the brain is the instrument, incommunicable knowledge. Galot speaks of an intuitive perception of God differing from the beatific vision afforded to the saints; this perception involves an intuitive knowledge of Jesus' own divinity. Rahner speaks of a self-awareness flowing from the hypostatic union, an unobjectified consciousness rather than an objective vision of the divine essence. Lonergan speaks of ineffable human knowledge, not obtained through corporeal or sensory action and not able to be manifested through such action.

that, if Jesus' knowledge was limited, his views are the views of his day and can be rejected by the much more learned twentieth century. A distinction is very necessary in response to such a contention, a distinction that needs to be emphasized not only for the "instant theologians" who read a little biblical exegesis and feel free to theorize, but also for some of the more formal theologians, especially in the field of moral theology. On the one hand, we have tried to indicate areas in which Jesus' views do seem to have been the limited views of his time. Perhaps these were areas in which he brought no new revelation to man, e.g., perhaps he had nothing new to say about the afterlife other than emphasizing what was already known, that God would reward the good and punish the wicked. On the other hand, we have indicated an area where his views were not at all those of his time, namely, the area of belief and behavior called for by the coming of the kingdom. And in this area, in my personal opinion, his authority is supreme for every century, because in this area he spoke for God. No age can reject the demand that one must believe in Jesus as the unique agent for establishing God's kingship over men (a uniqueness which the Church at Nicaea finally came to formulate in terms of Jesus' being "true God of true God"). No age can reject the harsh moral demands that Jesus made in the name of that kingship, no matter how much they may offend against "the common consent of good men." Thus, at least in the mind of this writer, a critical biblical evaluation of Jesus' knowledge takes nothing from his authority in that area which he made his own, the area of the kingdom of God.

But when all is said and done, the great objection that will be hurled again and again against any exegete (or theologian) who finds evidence that Jesus' knowledge was

limited is the objection that in Jesus Christ there is only
one person, a divine person. And so, even though the divine person acted through a completely human nature, any
theory that Jesus had limited knowledge seems to imply a
limitation of the divine person. Perhaps the best answer to
this objection is to call upon Cyril of Alexandria, that
Doctor of the Church to whom, more than to any other,
we are indebted for the great truth of the oneness of person
in Christ. It was that ultra-orthodox archfoe of Nestorianism (two persons or powers in Christ) who said of Christ,
"We have admired his goodness in that for love of us he
has not refused to descend to such a low position as to
bear all that belongs to our nature, INCLUDED IN
WHICH IS IGNORANCE."[92]

[92] PG 75, 369. We do not mean to suggest that Cyril grappled with
the problem of Jesus' limited knowledge in the way in which that
problem is treated today, but only that the admission which Cyril
makes is significant.

Epilogue:

THE RELEVANCE OF THESE QUESTIONS

"Relevance" is one of the clichés of our time; yet, while I firmly reject "relevance" as a criterion for all that should be learned, I do feel that it is an issue that should be part of the discussion of Jesus as God and man. After a lecture I gave on Jesus as God in the New Testament, a student asked me why the issue raised at Nicaea was so important. What difference did it make whether Jesus was God or the most perfect creature, so long as one accepted him as the Savior? I suppose the same type of question could be asked about Jesus' human knowledge, although the present generation is less likely to ask it in that regard. Behind these questions there is the suspicion that Nicaea and Chalcedon and indeed the whole christological controversy of the fourth and fifth centuries were matters of dipthongs (Homoousians vs. Homoiousians) and of bygone metaphysics that have no "relevance" today — a suspicion to which Bishop Pike's statements about the Trinity lend no little support. I could not disagree more; for I think that the questions we have discussed above, which are the byproducts of Nicaea and Chalcedon, are questions that concern the love of God for man.

If Jesus is not "true God of true God," then we do not know God in human terms. Even if Jesus is the most perfect creature far above all others, he can tell us only at second hand about a God who really remains almost as distant as the Unmoved Mover of Aristotle. This God may have been so thoughtful and loving as to take an interest in history and to send a Savior, but then it cost Him nothing in a personal way. Only if Jesus is of God do we know that God's love was so real that He gave Himself for us. Only if Jesus is of God do we know that it is of His nature to redeem the creation that He brought into being. Only if Jesus is of God do we know what God is like, for in Jesus we see God translated into terms that we can understand. This is why the proclamation of Nicaea was and is so important — not only because it tells us about Jesus, but because it tells us about God.[1] Indeed were it otherwise, the Nicene proclamation would scarcely be Christian, for Jesus did not come to preach himself but the kingship of God.

So also do I think that the proclamation of Chalcedon has enduring value, even for those who cannot pronounce Monophysitism. Unless we understand that Jesus was truly human, we cannot comprehend the depth of God's love. And if theologians should ultimately come to accept the limitations of Jesus' knowledge that we have seen reflected *prima facie* in the biblical evidence, then how much the more shall we understand that God so loved us that He subjected Himself to our most agonizing infirmities. A Jesus who walked through the world knowing exactly what the morrow would bring, knowing with certainty that three days after his death his Father would raise him up, is a Jesus who can arouse our admiration, but still a Jesus far from us. He is a Jesus far from a mankind that can only hope in the future and believe in God's goodness, far from a mankind that must face the supreme uncertainty of death with faith but without knowledge of

[1] On this point see the excellent treatment by D. M. Baillie, *God Was in Christ* (London: Faber Paperback, 1961), pp. 70–71.

what is beyond. On the other hand, a Jesus for whom the future was as much a mystery, a dread, and a hope as it is for us and yet, at the same time, a Jesus who would say, "Not my will but yours" — this is a Jesus who could effectively teach us how to live, for this is a Jesus who would have gone through life's real trials. Then would we know the full truth of his saying: "No man can have greater love than this: to lay down his life for those he loves" (Jn 15:13), for we would know that he laid down his life with all the agony with which we lay it down. We would know that for him the loss of life was, as it is for us, the loss of a great possession, a possession that is outranked only by love.

In the fourth and fifth centuries the question of Jesus as God and man was not an abstract question debated in the scholars' chambers; it was a question of what God and Christianity were all about. I submit that, if we take the trouble to understand, it remains all of that even in the twentieth century.

Scripture Index

107

Author Index

(This index does not include all the places an author's name is mentioned. It includes the places where bibliographical information is given, or where there are important discussions of an author's views.)